Other Books by M. Blaine Smith

REACH BEYOND YOUR GRASP: Embracing Dreams That Reflect God's Best for You — and Achieving Them

MARRY A FRIEND: Finding Someone to Marry Who Is Truly Right for You

EMOTIONAL INTELLIGENCE FOR THE CHRISTIAN

THE YES ANXIETY: Taming the Fear of Commitment

OVERCOMING SHYNESS: Conquering Your Social Fears

ONE OF A KIND: A Biblical View of Self-Acceptance

FAITH AND OPTIMISM: Positive Expectation in the Christian Life

GOAL SETTING FOR THE CHRISTIAN: Harnessing the Stunning Power of Focus and Persistence to Realize Your Potential for Christ — and Your God-Given Dreams

SHOULD I WAIT IN FAITH OR STEP OUT IN FAITH? Balancing Patience and Initiative in the Christian Life

KNOWING GOD'S WILL: Finding Guidance for Personal Decisions

SHOULD I GET MARRIED?

BEYOND STAGE FRIGHT AND INTO THE SPOTLIGHT: Overcoming Performance Anxiety and the Fear of Public Speaking — and Winning the Hearts of Your Audience

Turning
the
Page

Finding the Courage
for Major Life Change
and the Wisdom to
Reinvent Yourself

M. Blaine Smith

SilverCrest
B•O•O•K•S

© 2015 M. Blaine Smith

SilverCrest Books
Gaithersburg, Maryland

e-mail: scr@nehemiahministries.com
www.nehemiahministries.com

All rights reserved. No portion of this book may be reprinted in any form without written permission from SilverCrest Books.

Unless otherwise noted, all biblical quotations are from The Holy Bible, New International Version®, NIV®, 1984 edition, Copyright © 1973, 1978, 1984, 2011 by Biblica, Inc.™ Used by permission. All rights reserved worldwide.

Front cover image is a modified portion of the photo "Sunrise on the Dalton Highway in Alaska" by Kelly from Austin, US, and used by permission under the Creative Commons Attribution-Share Alike 3.0 Unported license [CC BY-SA 2.0 (http://creativecommons.org/ licenses/by-sa/2.0)], via Wikimedia Commons.

Biblical quotations marked RSV are from the Revised Standard Version of the Bible, copyright 1952 [2nd edition, 1971] by the Division of Christian Education of the National Council of the Churches of Christ in the United States of America. Used by permission. All rights reserved.

Library of Congress Control Number: 2015902701

ISBN: 978-0-692-39011-5

Author's Note

From time to time, we each face two types of major life change: that which we welcome and that which we don't. Unwelcome change is thrust upon us through a misfortune or setback of some sort—the death of a loved one, a romantic disappointment, a financial loss, a health crisis, a natural disaster, an unexpected job termination. Welcome change may be thrust upon us as well through a happy surprise: an inheritance, the discovery of treasure in our backyard, an unexpected job offer we can't refuse, the man or woman of our dreams who pursues us relentlessly. These are the exceptions with welcome change, though, and for most of us the rare aberration. Usually, we have to initiate that new opportunity we yearn for.

And here we face two challenges: We have to identify the new direction we ought to take with our life. And we have to find the courage to pursue it. These challenges are serious enough that I've devoted this book exclusively to welcome change; I hope to explore the challenges of unwelcome change and dealing with personal loss in another book.

There is, to put it simply, enough to be said about making welcome change to fill a book. Coming to grips with a certain new step we should take is challenging enough. Inertia is a powerful force in our experience, and we tilt strongly toward the status quo. We have to be keenly alert both to God's inspiration and to our own desires to recognize a new direction that's truly right for us. We'll look carefully at how to achieve this frame of mind, which, in short, requires substantial wisdom.

It can then take considerable courage to follow this new path. A host of concerns, ranging from fears of failure to fears of success, can trouble us and hold us back. Much of this book is devoted to how to master our fears, and how to distinguish reasonable concerns from unreasonable ones. My intent through all this discussion is to help you be fully open to the best new adventures God has for you.

Because I've addressed the topic of major life change in some of my previous books, I've borrowed or reworked certain portions from them in this one. Much of the material, though, is fresh, and you'll find many topics covered here that I haven't addressed in a book before. As a Christian writer, my concern tilts especially toward helping Christian readers find God's direction for their lives, and work through the unique issues we face as believers. But regardless of your faith, I believe you'll find our discussion relevant to the crossroads situations you face—and so I hope you'll give this book a chance, whether or not you agree with my spiritual stance. If you're longing to reinvent yourself in some way, or to find a new dream to embrace, I believe this book will help you do it.

Most of all, I hope you'll find my enthusiasm for taking on new adventures contagious, and our discussion inspiring you to become all that God has made you to be. I wish you his best as you read, and his wisdom and courage as you consider new directions for your life, and open yourself to his best options for your future!

Part One

Awakening to Your Need for Change

1

New Beginnings

It's hard to imagine anyone wanting to be married more than Lindsey. Not once during her teens or twenties, did her dream of being happily married ever waver. After several failed relationships, Lindsey finally met Elliot, and things clicked from the start. She was now 28.

For the next year, as they hung out and dated frequently, Lindsey grew more and more impressed with him. He was caring, compassionate, an exceptional listener, and a strongly supportive friend. He was also financially responsible, much loved by his friends, and—most important to Lindsey—a strong Christian.

When Elliot proposed on Valentine's evening, a Saturday, Lindsey readily accepted. On Sunday she jubilantly told her parents and many friends that she had finally realized her dream of finding a wonderful husband.

But Monday morning she awoke with a start. The thought of marrying Elliot suddenly filled her with dread, though she wasn't certain why. Her anxiety continued to spike the next few days, prompting her to reexamine her decision carefully. She only grew more convinced that Elliot was right for her. But why, then, this crippling anxiety? Why was she dreading what she wanted so deeply? Her friends all reassured her that Elliot wasn't the problem, and insisted he was ideal for her. They urged Lindsey to simply live through her commitment jitters and stay the course toward marriage.

After a few days, Lindsey's anxiety eased. In the weeks ahead she felt elated about marrying Elliot on some days, but panic-stricken on others. In late spring, on one of those easy days, she and Elliot set a wedding date, for September 15. They would mail the invitations August 1.

There were good days the next few months, but anxiety filled many others. On them Lindsey felt trapped at the thought of marrying—like being stuck in an elevator. Sometimes she would awake at night, so frightened of marrying she couldn't fall back asleep.

When the invitations arrived on July 25, Lindsey's panic went through the roof. To mail them out felt like no turning back, and on July 31 she told Elliot she just couldn't do it. As deeply as she wanted to marry him on one level, she felt too conflicted to go ahead. Perhaps later she would find the resolve to do it. For now, breaking their engagement seemed the only path to relief.

Our Mixed Emotions about Change
It is perhaps life's greatest irony that we can long for a certain change in our life greatly, even dream about it for years, yet dread the possibility just as strongly. We may fear the new milestone so much that we defeat our best efforts to achieve it, or fail to seize a golden opportunity to realize our dream. It's often this way with major improvements we envision for our life. This mixture of longing and dread, which Lindsey experienced, is common for many who entertain marriage, especially in the face of a compelling opportunity. I've counseled countless women and men who've long yearned to marry, but then are stunned to find themselves panicked and am-

bivalent when an enticing chance actually presents itself.

In this book I want to look carefully at a variety of fears that can hold us back, not only from marriage, but from other major changes we need to make, in our career and professional life, our living situation, our friendships, our church relationship, our lifestyle, and other important areas. Most important, I'll look at how we can confront and overcome these fears, and not let them hinder us from vital steps of faith we should take.

I'll also give close attention to how we can let go of the past, when we need to, in order to embrace God's best for our future. Major life change isn't just about embracing an unknown and sometimes intimidating future, but also about leaving the past behind— in many cases, a past that has owned our life so thoroughly that it's difficult to think of ever walking away from it. Yet sometimes a situation that feels familiar and comfortable is less than God's best for us.

Furthermore, life is far from an exact science. Each of us, as we navigate much unmapped terrain en route to realizing our potential, makes some good choices and some bad ones. And we make some that are right for us at one time but not another. We invariably come to points where we realize that a situation or a goal we've chosen to pursue just isn't working for us. Sometimes we discover that a dream we've devoted ourselves to earnestly doesn't fit us nearly as well as we had hoped. Yet a big part of us resists letting go of it, because we've staked our identity in it so strongly.

Jason is a gifted high school history teacher, loved by students for his ability to make an often dry subject interesting. Yet for years he pursued a legal career. Although Jason was a talented attorney, he wasn't out of law school long before he realized his passion for law was far less than that of his associates.

By his early 30s, he had determined that his strongest gifts and interests lay in teaching, not in fighting legal battles. The fact that he had long been fascinated with studying history led him to conclude he should teach that subject. And working with his church's youth ministry convinced him he would enjoy teaching high school students.

Deciding he ought to become a teacher was one thing. Mustering the courage to leave the legal profession was quite another, and it took him three years to do it. Changing careers not only meant disappointing his parents—who had urged him to become an attorney and financed his higher education—but admitting to others and himself that he had spent years chasing a dream that wasn't right for him. It also meant financial sacrifice—trading a liberal salary for a more modest one, and finding a way to fund further education. Jason worried, too, if he had the potential to be a good teacher, and whether he could find a position with a high school.

Today, his only regret is that he took so long to make this change. It has opened up a much more fulfilling career for him, and one that has proven to match his potential remarkably well.

Jason was fortunate in finally finding the courage to risk and shift careers. But many factors could have held him back, including his discomfort with changing his identity so sharply, his fear of disappointing his parents, his fear of failure, and simple pride. His example reminds us that, while it's easy enough to fantasize about reinventing ourselves, following through is another matter.

My Own Odyssey
In 1974, like Jason, I faced the challenge of the zebra changing its stripes. I was directing Sons of Thunder then, an early Christian rock band I had founded in 1967. It was the first active Christian rock band in the eastern United States, and the first to produce a nationally distributed album. Its concert opportunities grew to the point that we launched a full-time operation in the summer of 1972. SOT was enjoying a substantial ministry, with twelve people on our team—singers, musicians and staff.

I finished college and a seminary masters while working with SOT, though, and by 1973 was sensing that my primary calling was to teach rather than perform music. Speaking and teaching were now motivating me more than performing. I grew attracted to the idea of developing a teaching ministry that would help Christians find their niches and realize their personal potential. I applied to the doctor of ministry program at Fuller Theological Seminary, 3,000 miles away in Pasadena, California. My hope was to study God's guidance, and how we as Christians can best understand his will for us personally and follow it.

I grew eager to follow this new star, to develop a seminar on knowing God's will and write a book on the subject. Yet this would require leaving Sons of Thunder, and letting go of the musical identity that had defined my life for many years. I would also be letting down others in the band, who depended on my leadership, and I knew SOT might break up if I left. I would be defying the vision we had embraced as well. We had mused so often about how God had brought SOT together, blessed its ministry amazingly, and was very possibly calling us each to an enduring commitment to its mission. Leaving the band would mean admitting I'd had that assumption wrong.

And so I wrestled with making this change for about a year. The pull of this new vision finally won out, and in April 1974 I told the band I was resigning. Here's the most interesting part: Most others in SOT decided to follow my lead, to leave and pursue new paths for their own lives. And the band did break up by the end of that year. But now with many years of hindsight it's strikingly clear that, like me, most in SOT at that time weren't cut out for a lifetime commitment to music, but were more gifted for other pursuits. While I thought my resigning would hurt them and leave them adrift, it actually freed them to follow their own stars. The band was also able to disband at a time when its ministry had possibly peaked, and to maintain a highly positive legacy. It was an important lesson that many ministries are called to be significant for a time, but not forever.

My experience with shifting careers is far from the most dramatic story you'll ever hear about major life change. But it did give me considerable empathy with the struggles many go through in deciding to reinvent themselves in some way. And it demonstrates this vital lesson for each of us—that when God is calling us in a new direction, he's also influencing others as well, by changing their thinking in certain ways. And he may use you as a role model, to inspire others to take new steps with their lives. While you may fear you'll be hurting them by the change you're considering, chances are better you'll be helping them, by challenging them to grow, and inspiring them to pursue new horizons of their own.

The bottom line is that we need to view major life change as a journey of *faith*—faith that our new direction will be best for us, and best for many others as well.

Reinventing Yourself Can Rejuvenate Your Life

In this book I want to encourage you to be fully open to new beginnings that will improve your life. And I want to help you become more excited about the idea of reinventing yourself, and comfortable with doing it from time to time. I also want to challenge you to become more self-aware and inquisitive—to be continually alert to any situations in your life where you would benefit and better serve Christ by changing them, even radically. I'll also give you the best advice I can about how to overcome the fears and inhibitions that can hold you back from God's new options for you. In short, I want to help you understand when major change is needed in your life, and help you find the courage to make it.

We can be *too* eager for change, to be sure—too restless, unstable and flakey. God doesn't want us constantly jumping from one commitment to another, and each new situation we take on deserves a fair chance to prove itself. I recall a popular young man I knew who tired of new romantic relationships after a few months. The initial euphoria of any romance *always* starts to wear off after several months—this is normal, and part of the cycle of building a solid, lasting relationship. But he used it as a pretext for breaking off the relationship and looking for a new one, and he had an endless succession of short-term romances. This isn't God's pattern for any of us.

For most of us, though, the problem is quite the opposite. We grow too settled, too drawn in to our comfort zone. We become too concerned with security and too risk-adverse. We need a major life change from time to time to keep adventure alive. When Jesus spoke of giving us abundant life, he wasn't speaking of a secure life but an *adventuresome* one. And the lifestyle he spoke of means sometimes taking certain steps that from our standpoint seem risky and scary, but which have the potential to improve our life and our ability to make a difference in the world.

God has so designed human life that we are happiest, healthiest and most productive when adventure defines our life more than security. I will take this bet about your life, in fact: The times you've felt happiest, most gripped with purpose and thrilled to be alive, have been when you were setting forth on a major new venture. Once you were fully committed and moving forward—no turning back and your bridges burned—the sense of being on a grand escapade took over. And you felt like you were doing something you were placed on earth to accomplish. Am I right?

Such a time for me came in the summer of 1974, when, after leaving Sons of Thunder, Evie and I set out to drive across America to California. We were headed to Fuller Theological Seminary in Pasadena. My intent was to study the will of God as thoroughly as I could, to better prepare to teach and write on the subject. We camped out on the way, sleeping in a pup tent, and our subcompact sedan and outsized luggage carrier on its roof were so overpacked that one of the car's tires blew out the second day. As we drove across southern Arizona, the desert temperature reached 120F, and our car's engine began to overheat. Following the owner's manual, we switched on the heater, to cool the engine by drawing air across it. And the heat blowing on us through the vents was cooler than the air flowing in the windows from outside!

I was studying Biblical Hebrew as we cruised the nation's

highways (the perfect pursuit to brighten a cross-country drive!).
My acceptance at Fuller was conditioned on passing a two-semes-
ter Hebrew course crammed into an eight-week summer class. But
a speaking commitment delayed our drive west, and so I had to
start the class ten days late. The teacher agreed to let me do so—if
I wanted to live dangerously. But he strongly advised against it,
insisting the challenge was just too great.

His assumption I was doomed to fail only stimulated me to prove
myself. I was highly motivated to show I could master the material,
even starting late, and thoroughly enjoyed studying this complex
subject as Evie and I drove to California. I don't recall any time in
my life when I've felt more filled with hope and eager anticipation—not just for that class, but for the doors my time at Fuller
would open. That hope proved justified on all levels: I earned an A
in the Hebrew class, and my sojourn at Fuller paved the way for my
first book, *Knowing God's Will*, and a teaching ministry that has
lasted almost 35 years.

While this ministry has served up many joys of its own, nothing has compared with the exhilaration I felt during that drive to
Pasadena, and in my early days at Fuller, as I was first beginning to
reinvent myself.

There is, in short, nothing quite comparable to the sensation of
launching of a major life change. It almost seems to be a law of
human life that we need a new beginning from time to time to keep
our sense of adventure fully alive.

We need the occasional fresh start as well for the sake of our
growth and development. There's something about taking a new
direction with our life that causes us naturally to fire on eight cylin-
ders. We suddenly find ourselves capable of learning new material
and mastering certain talent we had previously thought too great a
stretch for us. I was never skilled at languages, for instance. I
struggled with French in high school, and had to drop a course in
classical Greek during my seminary masters, because I found the
subject too difficult. But I mastered basic Hebrew at Fuller—a more

difficult subject than French or classical Greek in certain ways—even with the serious disadvantage of starting that crash course ten days late. The reason I triumphed this time, I'm certain, is because my motivation was much higher.

While a major life change can stimulate us to grow in many ways, it also can pave the way for us to realize our greater potential over the long haul. The new beginning, in the best case, is an effort to redefine our life, to help it better align with who God has made us to be. Its aim is to help us more greatly use our gifts and talents, and to work more fully from natural motivation, that we might make a more significant contribution to human life.

Where We're Heading
I strongly hope this book helps you become alert to when a fresh start is recommended for you, and more eager to reinvent yourself when the time is right to do so.

Of course, you may have picked up this book precisely because you're facing a major life change, or are seriously considering one, and are looking for reassurance about what to do and the courage to take the plunge.

In either case, we'll look at many critical issues related to making a new beginning in the pages ahead.

In the rest of Part One (Awakening to Your Need for Change) I'll examine five major reasons we can miss the need for personal change—devoting a chapter to each. I'll stress how we can be most alert to the need to reinvent ourselves, and readily recognize golden opportunities to do so. Our topics will include—

Taking Your Dreams and Desires Seriously (chapter two). We can overlook the need for a certain change because we fail to appreciate the importance of our uniqueness—our special gifts, talents, personality and natural interests. I'll urge you to see yourself as a distinctive creation of God, and to let that understanding guide your decisions. This may mean shifting direction from time to time, in order to align yourself better with God's special intentions for you.

Self-Consistency (chapter three). Simple inertia also easily keeps us stuck in place, even when something better is beckoning us. We default toward seeing our future possibilities in terms of how our life is now. And we resist change in our self-image, even when it's in a positive direction—a tendency psychologists call "self-consistency." We'll examine this inclination, and how to keep it from limiting our growth.

Seeing Your Limitations as Strengths (chapter four). Dwelling too greatly on our limitations—real or imagined—can also discourage us from acting boldly. It's vital to focus much more on our strengths, and to let them inspire our decisions. Our limitations then so often end up benefiting us and becoming our allies. We'll look at different ways our limitations can actually help us achieve our dreams and improve our options.

Past Guidance and Present Decisions (chapter five). We can also get locked in to an outmoded understanding of God's will in some area of our life, which keeps us from recognizing a new direction he wants us to take. Or we fear we don't have permission to take it—that we would be violating a previous call from God to be where we are now. I'll explore this issue—a thorny one for some of us—and stress the importance of seeing God's will for our life dynamically.

Regretting the Choice That Seemed So Right (chapter six). Sensing we need to take a new direction with our life can create a unique personal crisis. We may wonder if we missed God's will in choosing to be where we are now. And if so, have we forsaken the chance to enjoy God's perfect plan for our future? That fear can dampen our incentive to seek his will anew and consider a major life change. The belief that we've been cast out of God's perfect plan, however, is always an overreaction. I'll explain why this is so, and how God's grace compensates for those occasions when we do make a truly bad decision.

In Part Two (Finding the Courage to Reinvent Yourself) we'll look more closely at the fears and hesitations that can hold us back

from a needed life change, even as we begin to recognize its importance for us. These apprehensions include—

The Fear of Failure (chapter seven). We fear we won't succeed, and are afraid to risk.

The Fear of Success (chapter eight). We worry that if we do
succeed, God will punish us for it, or we'll suffer other repercus-
sions.

The Fear of Commitment (chapter nine). We dread the thought
of being locked in to a certain role or responsibility, even though
we may have longed for it up till now. We feel panicky, trapped and
claustrophobic at the idea of firmly committing ourselves.

The Imposter Phenomenon (chapter ten). We fear we're unquali-
fied or unworthy to take on a certain responsibility or role—even
when it fits us well—and that some mortifying incident will expose
us to others as a fake.

I'll examine how each of these fears or concerns can thwart us,
even torture us, and keep us from important new adventures God
offers us. Most important, I'll offer counsel for conquering our apprehensions and finding the courage to seize life's best new opportunities.

Then in the final chapter, Pulling Up Roots, I'll look at one
further factor that can make it difficult to leave the past behind—
"the endowment effect" (we find it hard to let go of the past because we've indentified with it so strongly)—and stress three steps
we can take to stay fully open to life's best new options for us.

Finally, in an appendix section (Promises and Vows) I'll explore an issue that, if it happens to affect you, can be vexing. What
if you've made a promise to take a certain path with your life—a
death-bed pledge to a dying spouse not to marry again, for instance,
or a commitment to a missions agency to serve an extended period
somewhere—but then find that the position you've chosen doesn't
fit you well? Or you've vowed to God to devote your life to a certain lifestyle or mission that in time leaves you miserable. Are you
ever free to break such a promise and leave the unhappy situation?

There is, fortunately, hope for this predicament, and the possibility of changing course with a clear conscience. I'll examine this issue carefully, and offer a perspective that's grace-centered and liberating.

Moving Ahead

Whether you're seeking to clarify a new direction to take with your life, or to find the courage to move ahead, I hope you find the discussion in this book both enlightening and emboldening. I hope that as you read, you find yourself developing a more vibrant vision for your future, and gaining a more natural inclination to go for the gold in terms of your possibilities. And I hope our study inspires in you a greater willingness to risk, and to take those vital steps that so far have seemed intimidating to you. May God bless you richly as you read, and help you to embrace the new adventures he has in store for you!

2

Taking Your Gifts
And Desires Seriously

Obedience.

What comes to mind when you hear the word?

Knuckling under and doing your homework? Sitting quietly in class, when you badly want to punch the guy next to you? Standing rigidly at attention till the ROTC commander yells "at ease"? Dutifully filing a tax report and paying every penny? Boarding an airplane with fear and trembling to keep a professional commitment? Punching the clock faithfully to keep your job? Following your dentist's order and getting a root canal?

I'll take this bet. Whatever thoughts or images "obedience" conjures up for you are negative. It means doing what's necessary, but not fun.

From the earliest age, when we first begin to understand the most rudimentary language, "obey" quickly becomes an unwelcome term. It always means putting our instincts on hold to do someone else's bidding.

Obey your parents. Obey your sitter. Obey your older sister.

Obey your teachers. Obey your scoutmaster. Obey the crossing guard. Obey your coach. Obey your boss.

By the time we reach adulthood, we've been heavily programmed to think of obedience as unpleasant. That obeying is required in any situation means our natural inclinations are wrong, and following the rules is what matters.

Enter now the Christian life and our relationship with Christ. Following Christ, by definition, means *obeying* him. The importance of obedience is central to much preaching, teaching and discussion that we hear.

Most Christians, like ourselves, bring a cold-shower concept of obedience into their Christian walk. The result is that most teaching and discussion we hear about obedience is heavy on self-denial. To obey Christ means, by default, to deny our desires; often it means doing the precise opposite of what we're inclined to do.

Scripture has plenty to say about the hard side of obedience. Jesus spoke of the need to "enter through the narrow gate" (Mt 7:13), and taught that picking up our cross is at least a daily necessity (Lk 9:23). Obeying Christ often does require us to act against our desires.

Yet another level of obedience is stressed in Scripture that is far less appreciated by Christians, and seldom explained meaningfully in talks or writing on the subject. Obedience to Christ—to say it simply—can require us to take action that we *desire* to take, even to do what we most dearly wish. While it may seem strange to say that such action could require *obedience*, the truth is we are complex psychological creatures. We may long to take a certain step with our life, yet refrain for various reasons that are less than healthy.

Scripture, for instance, exhorts us frequently to use our gifts and talents. The implication always is that we'll experience joy and creative satisfaction in doing so. Yet Paul had to tell Timothy on one occasion to "stir up" the gift God had given him (2 Tim 1:6 KJV), and on another not to neglect his gift (1 Tim 4:14). While Timothy undoubtedly took great pleasure in his pastoral role, he was holding back for some reason. Obedience for him involved recapturing the thrill of using his special gift for ministry.

The Bible also stresses the importance of courting pleasure in the marriage relationship—as an act of obedience—and of stirring up affection for one's spouse. "Rejoice in the wife of your youth. . . . Let her affection fill you at all times with delight, be infatuated always with her love," the Proverb declares (Prov 5:18-19 RSV). Paul also instructs married couples to give significant attention to their sexual relationship (1 Cor 7:5). We find the strength to stay faithful in marriage, both writers stress, not through rigid self-denial, but by enjoying physical intimacy with our spouse. That relationship is an antidote to immorality, removing the temptation to seek an affair.

Then, speaking broadly about extending help to those in need, the writer of Hebrews urges, "let us consider how to stir up one another to love and good works" (Heb 10:24 RSV). We should make every effort to encourage compassion in each other, he is saying—so that acts of kindness will spring naturally from heartfelt concern for others' welfare and a desire to be helpful, rather than from grim obligation. Paul notes that this same eagerness should also govern financial giving, stressing that "God loves a cheerful giver" (II Cor 9:7).

Scripture, in short, highlights three areas where *stirring up enjoyment* is at the heart of obeying Christ most effectively: in using our gifts, in staying loyal in marriage, and in performing acts of mercy. The point is not that we can reach a stage where obedience is always fun and we are to obey only if we feel like it. Still, the highest level of obedience in the biblical view springs not merely from a sense of duty, but is joy-inspired.

Joy and Obedience
One reason this is true is that we're most productive when we're engaged in activity we deeply enjoy. We focus better on the task at hand, apply ourselves more energetically, and are more alert to others'

needs. Others are drawn to us more readily as well, and we have greater opportunity to help them.

We're also less susceptible to immorality when we're taking pleasure in the roles Christ wants us to assume. This is most obvious in the way our satisfaction in a good marriage reduces our temptation to seek an illicit relationship. Yet concentrating on work we love brings a similar benefit. When we're creatively stimulated, or delighting in helping others, our emotional energy is focused constructively, and wandering fancies have less room to develop.

This intriguing relationship of joy and obedience lays two priorities on us. We need, on the one hand, to do whatever is possible to stoke our enthusiasm for the responsibilities to which Christ calls us. Praying frequently that God will give us pleasure in using our talents, compassion for those in need, and joy in responding to their needs, can help us stay exuberant in all the roles where we exercise our gifts or help others. We should also seek the encouragement of supportive people who see our life positively; books, music, and leisure activities help to recharge our batteries as well. It's equally important, if we're married, to pray often that God will keep love and romantic chemistry substantial between us.

In addition to doing such things to keep our motivation strong, we need to make *choices* that allow our life to best reflect the gifts and aspirations God has put within us. And for each of us, this will mean from time to time making certain major changes in our life's direction, which allow it to conform better with who God has made us to be. It's here that obedience becomes most interesting. Picking up our cross at times can involve nothing less than committing ourselves to do what, underneath, we most earnestly want to do. I chose my language carefully, for while our *underlying* eagerness may be substantial, certain psychological factors can work against us— keeping us from appreciating what we most desire, or robbing us of the courage to go forward. Obedience comes in overriding these tendencies. We need to do our best to understand and overcome them, and, if necessary, to move ahead in spite of them.

In Part Two of this book, we'll look closely at five inhibitions that can keep us immobile even when golden opportunities present themselves. They include the fear of failure, the fear of success, the fear of commitment, the imposter phenomenon, and the endowment effect. In the remaining chapters of this section, we'll examine some other tendencies that can hold us back, including self-consistency, focusing too greatly on our limitations, and certain misconceptions about God's will. There are, as we'll see, *many* reasons we may resist doing what we want to do, and even sabotage our prospects for success. We may experience more than one of these issues, too. And, with so many possibilities, chances are good we'll feel at least some resistance to seizing the best opportunities life offers us.

We can do much to better understand our psychological makeup and to overcome fears and doubts that hinder our potential. We ought to take every practical step toward healing that we can. However, we always reach a point in the process where it's necessary to do what unsettles us in order to put our anxieties to rest. If we wait until all misgivings are gone, we'll wait forever, and important opportunities will pass us by.

It's here that obedience takes on its most therapeutic role. The fact that Christ *requires* me to take a certain step in the face of apprehension—especially when it's something I otherwise want to do—can give me exactly the incentive I need to go ahead. Knowing that "it's an order" breaks me beyond endless analysis of the "what-ifs," and simplifies the decision process incredibly.

Obedience in this case may mean changing careers, to a profession that better matches my potential and interests. Obedience comes in going ahead in spite of my fear of failing in this new career path, and worries that my finances won't survive the transition.

Obedience may also mean accepting the offer to teach a Sunday School class—something I've fantasized about doing, and underneath believe I would genuinely enjoy. Yet because I'm frightened of public speaking, obedience means doing it anyway, trusting that Christ will enable me to master my fears.

Obedience may also require me to go ahead and marry some-one I truly long to marry, and who I believe—in my most enlight-ened moments—is an excellent match for me, even though I feel increasingly panicky as the wedding day approaches. Obeying Christ means trusting he will hold me up through the engagement period and through the wedding, and grant a more joyful, stable experi-ence emotionally in this relationship once our vows are taken, and the decision to marry is fully behind me.

Designer Fashioned
The most thrilling part of this concept of obedience is that it gives us a basis, even a mandate, for taking our abilities and desires seri-ously. Many Christians feel squeamish devoting themselves to work they're naturally skilled for, out of fear it will prevent them from fully trusting Christ. Better to take on responsibility you're less capable of handling, they insist, so you'll be compelled to depend on Christ to give you the ability you need and positive results. Yet following the path of our talent is often the most seriously chal-lenging step we can take, given the host of fears, tendencies and concerns that can stand in our way. We typically have a stronger basis for trusting Christ working within our natural potential than outside of it.

In the same way, many Christians are uneasy basing major de-cisions on their desires, for fear of taking the easy course—not "en-tering by the narrow gate"—and bowing to the desires of the flesh. "The heart is deceitful above all things," Jeremiah reminds us (Jer 17:9). Yes, the heart is unquestionably deceptive in *moral* matters, and each of us has certain behavioral areas where we must always be watchful and exercise restraint. But when it comes to major de-cisions involving our talents, potential and long-term commitment of our time, we most glorify God by *following* our desires. They give us a vital insight into how God has created us, and into how we can live in the center of his will. And as we all discover, following their path is often difficult, given all the inhibitions we face. Pursuing a dream we long to realize typically challenges us to trust Christ more fully than taking a less appealing course.

We should regard it as a matter of stewardship, then, to have a keen self-understanding—of our talent, potential and natural interests—and to respect it in our turning-point decisions. We should assume God hasn't made a mistake in fashioning us uniquely as he has, and that more than any other factor, our self-understanding will enlighten us to how he wants us to invest our life.

An important question remains, however, and that is whether the self-understanding that should guide us should include the potential and natural interests present throughout our life, or only after we become a Christian. Does God grant me new abilities and a new personality once I become a believer, and refashion me in such a way that I should disregard everything that has come before now? Let's say I become a Christian at age 25. Up to now I've discovered a talent for managing a business, and a strong desire to be an entrepreneur, plus a long-standing desire to be married with a family. Do these inclinations have any bearing on what God wants me to do now, or are they irrelevant?

Spiritual Gifts

Scripture does speak of God's giving us new talent when we become a Christian—what the New Testament terms "spiritual gifts" (Rom 12:3-8, 1 Cor 12—14, Eph 4:7-14). Paul explains that spiritual gifts are given "for the common good" (1 Cor 12:7), that is, the good of the body of Christ. My spiritual gift is an ability that enables me to support, encourage, build up and/or challenge other Christians. As such, it may be an ability in an area where I've always had potential, and often is. This isn't always the case, though, and some, once Christian, discover a completely new talent they've never been aware of before.

And so someone who has never taught nor had any inclination to teach finds she's highly effective teaching within the church.

Another with no prior speaking experience finds he's gifted as a preacher. Yet another, who was selfish and contentious before becoming Christian, is now blessed, to everyone's surprise, with a gift of mercy.

These transformations happen, and each of us should strive to understand how we can best serve the body of Christ. We discover our spiritual gift—or *gifts*, if we're so fortunate—in the same way we do our other talent, by *experimenting*. We look for what we're most productive doing, and what we most enjoy doing that helps other Christians. When we find that magic combination of effectiveness and joy, we've likely pinpointed a spiritual gift. That discovery can be one of the most thrilling of the Christian life.

That said, two things are critical to understand about the spiritual gift. One is that it doesn't replace other ability we have but adds to it. We continue to enjoy the same talent and potential we've always possessed. Priscilla and Aquila, along with Paul, continued to be tent makers after their conversion to Christ, for instance.

Also, there's no evidence whatever in the New Testament that most Christians are expected to build a career out of a spiritual gift, nor that we should think of that option as an ideal to strive for. Indeed, it appears most New Testament Christians didn't base their profession on a spiritual gift, but continued in their previous line of work, while using their spiritual gift to support their church. I would strongly caution you, in fact, not to try to fashion a career out of a spiritual gift unless you're certain it's the path you're most gifted and motivated to follow. You need strong evidence, too, that focusing on your gift full-time won't lessen your effectiveness or joy in using it. It's in this sense that the longtime pastor of Philadelphia's Tenth Presbyterian Church, Donald Grey Barnhouse, is reported to have counseled, "Don't become a pastor if you can possibly avoid it."

Our spiritual gift is, though, a vital part of our total mix of potential, and will sometimes strongly influence a turning-point decision. As our other talent sometimes does, it will mandate us to take a challenging step with our life—a change in direction that allows us to use our spiritual gift more effectively. For a much fuller discussion of spiritual gifts and the responsibilities they lay on us, I strongly recommend C. Peter Wagner's classic, *Your Spiritual Gifts Can Help Your Church Grow*,[1] which remains the best book I've come across on the subject.

Do We Get a New Personality as a Christian?

A more confusing question for many believers is whether God puts a new personality in us when we become a Christian. No one would question that God thoroughly reworks us internally once we choose to follow Christ. But does this mean I'm no longer the distinct individual I was before giving my life to Christ? Is my individuality now annulled? And has God replaced it with a new personality of his choosing?

If I am still the same individual, does God want me to override that? Is personality something objective for the Christian, and is there an ideal Christian personality I should strive for? Does God want me to deny my individuality, so that it doesn't interfere with what Christ is doing in me?

Or—does the truth lie at the other extreme? Does God want me to affirm my individuality now that I'm a Christian, and to nurture those factors that have long made me unique?

Ideas abound in so many Christian circles about the "ideal Christian personality," and this is a major reason for our confusion. While it may not be taught explicitly that one personality type is more godly than another, stereotypes persist nonetheless. Many Christians assume that leaders and other strong believers they admire are closer to having the perfect Christian personality than they themselves.

As a new Christian, I simply assumed that the extroverted leaders of our church college group, with their football coach temperaments, were displaying God's personality standard. I disdained my own personality, which seemed too mild and reflective compared to theirs, and did what I could to emulate the personality style of these leaders I esteemed.

Our confusion about individuality also results from certain theological misconceptions about what it means to a have new life in Christ. Scripture teaches that we're new creations as Christians. We're urged to deny our old nature and die to ourselves, in order to be fully alive in Christ. From there, it's an easy jump to thinking we must deny what's unique about our own personality and potential in order to be Christlike.

Personality Change vs. Character Change

There's no question that God wishes to change our lives once we're Christian. And we're clearly expected to exercise plenty of self-denial. But what is it he wishes to change? And what are we expected to deny?

It may seem natural to assume God wants to change our personality, and wants us to deny those personal traits that make us unique. Yet, in fact, he isn't concerned with changing our personality so much as our *character.* He doesn't wish to radically modify our personality, but to *redirect* it. Few distinctions are more important to appreciate in the Christian life, and few contribute more to our productivity.

Here it's extremely helpful to understand how the New Testament uses certain Greek words that refer to the psychological dimensions of human life. These terms include *kardia*—the heart, or seat of one's emotions; *nous*—the mind or will; *suneidêsis*—the conscience; and *psychê*—the soul, or life of an individual. These words appear numerous times throughout the New Testament, referring to both Christians and non-Christians alike. Every individual has these qualities, whether they are Christian or not.

What is interesting is that the New Testament never states that the Christian receives a new *kardia, nous, suneidêsis* or *psychê*. It speaks of the *kardia* being purified (Acts 15:9, Jas 4:8), the *nous* being renewed (Rom 12:2, Eph 4:17), the *suneidêsis* becoming good

(1 Pet 3:16, 21), and the *psychê* being saved (Heb 10:39, Jas 1:21, 1 Pet 1:9). But it is always *my* heart that is purified, *my* mind that is renewed, *my* conscience that is good, *my* life that is saved. The New Testament never implies, though its use of these terms, that God implants a new psychic existence into one who becomes a believer.

The New Testament does describe the believer as having a new life. But here the word it uses is always *zôê*—which refers not to an individual's distinctive inner life, but to *a quality of life* that all Christians enjoy. The Christian is one who has a new dimension of life, which Scripture often calls eternal life. Its use of *zôê* to denote this new life in no way implies a change in one's psychological uniqueness, but rather a change in morality, motivation, desires, priorities, behavior, and so on.[2]

Paul, as a Christian, Was Still an Individual

Thus, when the New Testament describes someone both before and after becoming a Christian, we find that the person's personality stayed intact after choosing to follow Christ. While considerable change took place in that person's life, he or she still remained the same individual—only now bent toward doing God's will, rather than toward acting against it.

Take Paul, for example. Before his conversion on Damascus road, he is shown as an extraordinary man of action and a superb leader. He didn't simply muse about persecuting Christians—he did something about it! He was also a man of exceptional intellectual capacity, who studied under Gamaliel—one of the chief Jewish scholars of the time (Acts 22:3). Neither of these qualities was annulled after he became a Christian, but simply propelled in a new direction. He became the chief firebrand in the young church's outreach mission, and a prime spokesman on Christian doctrine.

Not that great change didn't occur in Paul's life after his conversion. He went through extensive transformation both spiritually and morally. He was no longer intent on murdering his religious enemies, for instance. The whole orientation of his life altered. But this character change didn't annihilate his personality so much as bring it into line with God's purposes.

Martha Was Still Martha after Coming to Faith

Among women in the New Testament, Martha is a fascinating example of someone who retained her individuality after she came to faith in Christ. Most of us have a negative impression of Martha. When we think of her, we recall the incident in Luke 10:38-42, when Jesus comes to her home for dinner. Martha busies herself with preparing the meal, while her sister, Mary, sits attentively at Jesus' feet listening to him. Finally, Martha, exasperated that Mary isn't helping her, blurts out to Jesus, "Lord, don't you care that my sister has left me to do the work by myself? Tell her to help me."

Jesus replies, "Martha, Martha . . . you are worried and upset about many things, but few things are needed—or indeed only one." We typically conclude that Jesus upbraids Martha for paying too much attention to practical details while neglecting more important personal matters. The lesson, we assume, is that Mary has the ideal Christian personality, and those of us who are like Martha should modify our personality to become more like Mary.

Yet the New Testament has more to say about Martha. Several days after her brother Lazarus dies, Jesus comes to console the family. Martha undergoes a profound spiritual transformation through talking with Jesus, and then witnesses him resurrect Lazarus (Jn 11). Sometime after this Jesus attends another dinner hosted by Martha (Jn 12:1-3). Since Martha's faith in Christ has grown considerably since the first meal, we might assume her personality is markedly different now, especially at the point she was so rough-edged before—her meticulous attention to detail. She'll now be following Mary's pattern of relaxing socially with Jesus, and letting others handle the food preparation.

Instead, John notes that "Martha served," while Mary again socializes with Jesus. Martha is *still* concentrating on preparing the meal! Yet now no mention is made of her being irritated with Mary for not helping. Hopefully, John's silence on this point means Martha doesn't criticize Mary this time, and has grown more accepting of Mary for who she is. If so, then Martha's spiritual growth has brought important character change. But what's abundantly clear is that Martha is still being Martha, still focused on the details of hosting. Her personality remains the same!

Being Yourself in Christ

The point we're making, then, is one of the most liberating we can embrace in the Christians life. The God who knew us before the foundation of the world (Eph 1:4), and saw us in our mother's womb (Ps 139:13), has placed in each of us a unique personality, within us from the moment of birth and intact throughout our life—present before we commit our life to Christ and remaining thereafter. There is no ideal Christian personality style we're expected to emulate. Instead, God has given us each a distinctive personality, which he wishes us to express and not repress as we follow Christ. This means we'll naturally gravitate toward doing certain things with our life; certain responsibilities and roles will appeal to us much more than certain others. And this is how God intends it!

God, as we've stressed, has also given us each the potential for developing certain talent. He may add to it with a spiritual gift or two after we become a Christian, bestowing ability on us we hadn't previously enjoyed. Yet our potential remains largely intact throughout our life; we find we're naturally more capable of certain tasks than certain others, even though that capability always requires development—in some cases years of devoted effort to fully harvest.

We should regard it as a matter of stewardship, then, to strive to understand our distinctiveness as thoroughly as possible. Dreams that have stood the test of time will often give us our best insight into what God wants us to do, especially when they combine with ability and potential we clearly possess.

For most of us, though, our best self-insight comes not in a blinding flash, but grows slowly and incrementally over time, from much experience and trial and error. Almost inevitably, too, we each come to certain points when we recognize a new direction we should take with our life, to allow it to better reflect the uniqueness God has given us and the special opportunities that cross our path. But as passionate as we may be on one level to make this change, our fears and inhibitions may be strong enough to hold us back.

It's here that our concept of obeying Christ makes a huge difference. If I believe he *requires* me to follow this new path, that may be the tipping point, giving me the heart to confront my fears and go ahead. And so I challenge you to embrace this way of thinking about obeying Christ—that on certain vital occasions, including your life's most important turning points, it will mean following your passion, and pursuing a dream that ignites you. This concept of obedience makes sense as we begin to appreciate just how challenging following the desires of our heart can sometimes be, and how greatly we need the Lord's wisdom and strength to do it.

3

Self-Consistency

No words can describe my sense of embarrassment and panic. *I'm at the end of a college semester. I've suddenly discovered that there are several courses I've simply forgotten to attend. Finals begin in a few days, and term papers are due. It's too late to withdraw with a passing grade. Should I make a heroic effort to get through, or just give up?*

It's a recurring dream that haunts my night from time to time. When I wake up, I remind myself that everything is all right. I made it through college long ago, and then went on to earn two graduate degrees. I never forgot to attend class for a week, let alone a semester.

Never mind. As much as I remind myself, the dream still recurs more often than I like to admit.

I have another recurring dream that is similar. One of the bands with which I used to play has come back together for a reunion concert. We're getting ready to go on stage and face a large audience. But we realize that we haven't rehearsed and are totally unprepared to perform.

Again, my experiences with musical groups have all been posi-tive ones. Still, the dream suggests that part of me has never moved beyond early fears of failure. . . .

I doubt a month goes by when I don't experience both of these dreams.

I quote this passage from my *One of a Kind,* with some adapta-tion.[1] It describes two recurring dreams I had long been having when, in 1983, I wrote that book. More than thirty years have now passed, during which these dreams have often returned. While they may not recur as frequently anymore, they still invade my night from time to time.

As I've shared about these dreams in talks and seminars, many have told me that their dream experience is similar. Long-ago col-lege graduates confess to suffering a similar recurring dream of academic disaster. And many admit they dream often of failure in other areas where they've long succeeded.

This may well be your experience too. But if not, just ask sev-eral friends at random, and you'll likely find one or more admits to often having such a dream.

What these dreams demonstrate is how truly hard it is to change the image we carry of ourselves. We may reach a major goal and enjoy a notable accomplishment, one we imagined would radically improve our self-image and boost our self-esteem. Yet to a surpris-ing degree, we continue to view ourselves as we were before this milestone, and continue to feel the same insecurities. We instinc-tively resist change in our self-image—even when it's in a positive, cherished direction.

Psychologists have a term for it: "self-consistency." While we have a strong drive to improve our self-image, we also have a sur-prisingly strong drive to maintain a *consistent* self-image, even if it means holding on to certain negative perceptions of ourselves.

Slow Growing

One repercussion of this inertia in our self-image is that we can be slow to fully absorb important lessons God is teaching us. Spiritual growth is typically a slow and challenging process. Growth in the way I think about God usually involves change in how I think about myself.

Developing a deeper trust in Christ's power, for instance, means growing in my conviction that I am important to Christ, that he loves me enough to meet my needs, and that he wants to express his power through me to meet the needs of others. If my self-image is poor, I may find it hard to believe that God could love me this extraordinarily. And the yen for self-consistency can provide powerful resistance to such a change in perspective.

We see this problem often illustrated by Jesus' disciples in the Gospels. Time and again, Jesus put them through experiences that taught them lessons not only about God but about themselves— that God's power wasn't just an abstract force, but something they were chosen to receive.

They were slow to catch on. In Mark 8:1-8, they face the immense problem of feeding themselves and a crowd of over four thousand people. Jesus responds by giving them a few loaves and fishes, and with these meager provisions they miraculously feed themselves and the hungry multitude. At the time, the disciples must have been awestruck by Jesus' uncanny power. And they must have been profoundly convinced of his desire to use his power to meet their needs and the needs of others through them.

A few hours later, that conviction is already lost. They are out in a boat with Jesus, desperately concerned about where their next meal is coming from! Jesus, referring to the miracle they've just experienced, asks them, "Why do you discuss the fact that you have no bread? Do you not yet perceive or understand? Are your hearts hardened? . . . And do you not remember?" (Mk 8:17-18 RSV).

It seems the disciples experienced stunning self-consistency in this incident, totally losing sight of how Christ had previously provided for them, and perceiving themselves no differently than before he began to transform them, but as ones untouched by the power of God. Of course, we identify with them all too easily. So often the hardest-won lessons in our Christian experience have to be relearned again and again. As I once heard a wise seminary professor put it, "We don't learn anything new in the Christian life; we just learn the same lessons over and over."

Turning Point Decisions

Just as self-consistency can be a drag on our spiritual life, slowing our growth and keeping us from fully learning important lessons, it can blind us to golden opportunities to improve our life. Taking a new direction with my life means changing how I think about myself. It means embracing a new self-image. And yet my self-image wants to stay static; it defaults to its longtime norm. In this sense, self-consistency is a rock under which we live, and without a serious effort to break through into the daylight, we're likely to miss welcome new horizons that await us.

In addition to our self-image being inert, we tend to view our life's broader circumstances statically. We default toward seeing our life as it is now. In the same way, we envision our future strongly in terms of our current circumstances. "What you see is all there is," Daniel Kahneman stresses throughout his popular book *Thinking, Fast and Slow*.[2] By that he means that our present circumstances strongly color our view of everything else. Our musings about the future are based much more on current information, however scant, than on potentially much more accurate data we don't yet have.

If I'm in an unhappy relationship, for instance, it's difficult to see beyond this sad circumstance and appreciate how I might feel in a different relationship sometime in the future, with this current one just a faint past memory. I'll default toward thinking this present relationship is the best available for me, rather than think more creatively about my possibilities. This is a further way self-consistency works to keep us in place.

We see this self-defeating mindset displayed by the lame man in John 5:1-15, who lay endlessly by the Pool of Bethesda, waiting for an angel to stir the waters. Jesus approaches him and asks, "Do you want to get well?" Of course he did! Why would Jesus possibly raise the question?

The man's response reveals why. "I have no one to help me into the pool when the water is stirred. While I am trying to get in, someone else goes down ahead of me." The lame man couldn't see beyond his current depressing situation; he assumed what he saw was "all there is." While he certainly wanted to be healed on one level, he wasn't embracing the thought of a better life as a realistic option. Self-consistency kept him immobile. When Jesus asked if he wanted to be healed, he implied the man needed a more vibrant vision for his future, which begins by wanting that outcome strongly.

In the same way, self-consistency can keep us too focused on our current unhappy circumstances. It can dull our thinking about new possibilities, and keep us from recognizing doors that are open. How, then, can we manage self-consistency effectively? How can we grow more fully alert to the new options God has for us, and embrace a more dynamic vision for our future?

Here are some steps that can help.

1. *Know yourself.* If you're reserved by nature, shy, conservative in how you live, obsessed with security and unnerved by risk, rooted in the same region and career for a long time, chances are inertia is blinding you to some important opportunities. Be aware of that and ready to compensate. Assume by default that God has more in store for you than you're seeing right now. Take heart from that hope if certain situations in your life are discouraging. If you're tending to despair over them, remind yourself that self-consistency may be coloring your thinking, and keeping you from seeing the broader picture. Stay hopeful for a better future, and follow these further steps.

If, on the other hand, you have a strong sense of adventure, have embraced a number of new ventures over the years, have tried different jobs, have enjoyed a fair number of friendships and relationships, have been flexible about where you live, have seized new opportunities when offered them, then self-consistency is less likely a serious problem for you.

2. Stoke your sense of adventure. If inertia tends to control your life, and you tilt too greatly toward security, push yourself to be more adventuresome. Vacation at a new spot. Take on a new sport or pastime. Venture into a new social group, at a church or elsewhere. Get out more than rarely to concerts, theater productions, sporting events, and festivals. Move to a new location. Join a gym and strive to be a fitness nut. Volunteer at a local shelter or YMCA. Offer to tutor an at-risk child. Keep fresh experiences occurring. We need a certain amount of *contrast*, of breaking with the familiar, to keep our mind stimulated and open to broader new possibilities for our life.

3. Strive to be proactive. If there's a situation in your life that's unsatisfying or unproductive, and has been for some time, don't simply wait for the skies to part and an angel to appear with instructions about what to do. Take serious initiative to study your options and find a solution. Remind yourself constantly that you should be *proactive* in finding a solution. The vocabulary we use in our "self-talk" truly makes a difference in how we think and live, and "proactive" is one of these powerful modern words that has a way of prodding us and boosting our optimism. It stirs us to realize, *Oh, yeah. There probably is something I can do to remedy this predicament. I'm likely missing a good solution and need to be more vigilant in finding it.*

If you're in a job that's frustrating, not paying you fairly or not tapping your potential well, actively explore the alternatives. Get the best help you can in finding a better position—if possible, a "headhunter" (employment agent) experienced with your profession who has a good track record. And don't discount the possibility of changing your career. If you have any inkling whatever toward a different career path, thoroughly research that option and look carefully at what you would have to do to reinvent yourself.

If you're single wanting to marry, don't assume that because you're a certain age and still unattached, God must want you to remain forever single. Assume God wants you eventually to marry, even if his timing is different for you than certain others, and thoroughly explore the options for meeting singles in your area. Phone every fair-size church you can find within 45 minutes of your home, or scour its web site, and find if it has a singles ministry worth investigating. Visit the most promising groups and discover firsthand what they have to offer. Research other singles organizations and activities in your region, and strive to identify the best opportunities for meeting marriage prospects. Then take good advantage of these options. Also join as least one major online dating service, and work its program. Diversify your options!

Don't let self-consistency numb your senses and keep you from thinking creatively about your future. Counteract this tendency by being proactive, by taking serious initiative. Carefully search for the best opportunities in your career, relationships and other areas, and do those things that open your mind and heart most fully to seeing new possibilities. Then earnestly pursue your most appealing options.

4. Associate with those who see your life dynamically. I mentioned earlier that for much of my twenties I directed the early Christian rock band Sons of Thunder. The idea to begin this band, though, wasn't my own but that of a visionary friend. I was a new Christian then, attending Fourth Presbyterian Church in Bethesda, Maryland. For eight years previously I had directed two local rock bands and played guitar with them, including the popular Newports. But shortly after giving my life to Christ, I left the Newports and stopped performing. I didn't expect to play music on a serious level again—it simply wasn't on my radar now—and I wanted to keep my time free for Christian activities and spiritual growth.

But Russ Cadle, Fourth Presbyterian's youth director, had a different idea. The church had a thriving college ministry, and Russ suggested I form a band to play for its events, which would present the gospel through contemporary music. That was remote from anything I imagined doing then. The concept seemed bizarre, too, for I wasn't aware of a Christian rock band existing anywhere. But because I respected Russ and trusted his judgment, I agreed to give it a try. The rest is history.

In this case, Russ saw my potential and my possibilities better than I did, and I'm forever grateful, both for his posing the idea and for encouraging me to pursue it. I would likely have missed this golden opportunity completely apart from his insight.

This is just one of many examples I could share of how a visionary friend helped me grasp the need to take an important step with my life. It's hard to exaggerate how greatly we benefit from being with those who see us dynamically, and naturally inspire us to reach new horizons. If you don't associate with such people often, I urge you to seek out at least one friend who has a knack for seeing your potential well, who is optimistic about you and thinks creatively about your possibilities. Your best source for finding this person is often a church, where you have the opportunity to make new friends by joining a class, Bible study or small group. Log time with this person as frequently as you can, and actively seek his or her advice about your future. Of course, if you can make several such friends, the more the better.

As much as you can, too, avoid being around negative people, especially those who cannot see you creatively, but hold to a static or outdated picture of you. Remember that Jesus himself had to break the bounds of his hometown Nazareth, where people still viewed him as an adolescent—even in his thirties!—and failed to fully grasp his unusual calling. "'Isn't this the carpenter? Isn't this Mary's son and the brother of James, Joseph, Judas and Simon? Aren't his sisters here with us?' And they took offense at him," Mark tells us (Mk 6:3). He adds, "He could not do any miracles there, except lay his hands on a few sick people and heal them" (Mk 6:5).

In the same way, too much time around unimaginative people can stifle your optimism and your ability to envision new options for your life. Seek out those who are farsighted by nature and who instinctively see your potential. If you have difficulty finding such people, seriously consider hiring a professional life coach, whom you meet with regularly, perhaps once or twice a month. While this involves some cost, the long-term return on this investment can be considerable.

I'm hard-pressed, in fact, to think of anything that jolts us out of self-consistency better than a visionary-thinking person who takes a sincere interest in us. The insight and encouragement of this individual can stimulate our imagination to see new paths for our life we haven't even considered, and to find the heart to pursue them.

5. *Make a habit of assuming what you see isn't all there is.* If no new horizon has enticed you for some time, assume one may be out there that God wants you pursue, which you haven't recognized yet, or which may become apparent soon. Make it part of your self-talk to remind yourself of this possibility often. Recall too that God wants to keep your life adventuresome. Just as sitting too long without standing up and moving around is harmful to your health, staying too stationary in your activities—espccially in their full mix—can render you less fulfilled and productive than God intends. Remind yourself of the benefits of keeping your life in motion.

Making these reminders can help stimulate your mind to muse about new possibilities. You should make them lightheartedly, and not self-condemningly, to be sure. God may or may not have a new path for you to follow at this time, and you simply want to stay open to any signals. You should never force yourself to take on a new venture simply for the sake of adventure, nor be swayed by a grass-is-greener mentality to try to milk more from life than you truly need. But having a new dream to pursue in at least some area of your life from time to time is generally healthy, and so it's a matter of balance. Reminding yourself that God may have more in store for you than you're seeing can help you stay more alert to new options.

6. *Give generous time to envisioning your future.* Devote significant time in the course of a year to reflecting on your future, and

considering new directions God might want you to take. Give at least a few minutes each week to such musing. Then at least every six months, devote a more substantial period to visionary thinking—a few hours, an afternoon, or preferably a full day—and think of this time as a personal retreat. Begin by praying earnestly that God will direct and inspire your thinking. Then simply relax and ponder your life, past, present, and especially future options that appeal to you. Allow generous time for God to "get your ear," and for any new dream that might be lurking beneath the surface to emerge. The benefit of this reflective time can be immense, and on occasion may even include an "aha moment," when you're stunned to recognize a compelling new direction you've never considered for yourself before.

7. Pray daily for victory over self-consistency. Finally, take at least a moment each day to pray that God will help you avoid the pull of self-consistency, as it might hinder your spiritual growth, choices for the day ahead, and decisions about your life's long-term direction. Pray too that God will enable you to grasp any new intention he has for you, and make you fully open to his inspiration.

One of the ironies of self-consistency is that it can dull our awareness of the power of prayer, and so we fail to take this vital step to combat self-consistency's impact. We can be profoundly convinced of prayer's potential on occasion, when a request is bountifully answered. But that conviction can slacken quickly and fade to a distant memory when we face a new challenge even a short time later. To paraphrase the oft-quoted investment disclaimer, past success in prayer is no guarantee of future performance. That is, a past victory doesn't assure we'll continue to take prayer seriously.

And so some discipline in our prayer life is essential, for we can't assume that just praying when we're moved to will be sufficient. We benefit tremendously from having a daily period committed to prayer and Bible study, as the focus of our spiritual growth. During this time, we should make a habit of asking for victory over self-consistency, plus alertness and openness to God's guidance.

This practice, along with other steps we take to grow spiritually, will greatly help us to turn the tide with self-consistency. We should take heart that while self-consistency is a powerful force, the nurture of God's Spirit in us is more powerful still. We take this reassurance from Jesus' disciples, who in time substantially overcame self-consistency, and developed a much healthier view of both God and of themselves.

What I find most encouraging is that Jesus didn't give up on his disciples when they continued to forget the lessons he had taught them. Rather, he patiently prodded them to recall their past experiences, and to apply what they had learned to their new challenges. He continued to query them in the boat, "'When I broke the five loaves for the five thousand, how many baskets full of broken pieces did you take up?' They said to him, 'Twelve.' 'And the seven for the four thousand, how many baskets full of broken pieces did you take up?' And they said to him, 'Seven.' And he said to them, 'Do you not yet understand?'" (Mk 8:19-21 RSV)

In the same way, Christ bears with us, continuing to remind us of the things we've learned but too quickly forgotten. It's in this sense that he promised the Holy Spirit will "bring to your remembrance all that I have said to you" and will "guide you into all the truth" (Jn 14:26, 16:13 RSV). By declaring that the Holy Spirit will *guide* us into truth, he implied it will be a process, not something that happens all at once.

We may be confident that as we seek to make the Lord first in our life and pray regularly for his help, he will in time enable us to triumph over self-consistency. How ever persistent its force is within us, his faithfulness is even more so—and that ultimately makes the difference.

4

Seeing Your Limitations
As Strengths

I have only a vague memory of him: he was an enormous man who dwarfed me. Of course, to a four-year-old, all adults are mammoth. He died that year, and that's the memory I carried of him from that point on—my grandfather as a towering giant.

A huge photo portrait in my parents' attic that I long assumed was of him reinforced the impression.[1] The man's face is large—Newt Gingrich-like—and you assume a substantial body lurked below.

I knew my grandfather was a career policeman, highly respected on the Washington, D.C. force, who rose to the position of assistant chief. My parents spoke of his love for police work, his success as an officer and his toughness with criminals—a stature in life that magnified my impression of him as a Big Man.

I don't recall them ever speaking specifically of his physical stature, though. Why, I'm not certain; I can only guess it wasn't relevant to their impression of him.

It *was* relevant to many others, I was fascinated to discover in

2000, some fifty years after his death and my last encounter with him. While Evie and I were cleaning out the attic of my mom's home, to prepare it for sale, we came across a scrapbook of news articles related to my granddad's police work and personal life. Many mention him by name; others detail events that were important to him. The collection is huge—several hundred pieces, spanning about twenty years, beginning with several articles on his wedding in 1909.

The articles confirmed my assumption about his character: he was a courageous policeman who tackled the tough assignments.

They challenged my visual image of him, though—substantially.

The first indication it needed adjusting came in an article early in the scrapbook describing my grandfather's efforts to toughen D.C.'s traffic legislation. The title: "Shorty Smith: Least of Cops in Size, Away Up in Traffic Laws."

Oh.

Many pieces that follow make reference to the fact that Captain Milton D. Smith, a.k.a. Shorty, was not only a man of unusually small stature, but *the shortest* policeman on the D.C. force.

So much for my image of Hulk Hogan.

There are photos with captions noting his status as the smallest cop, and references to his stature in various articles reporting his activities. The distinction finds its way into article titles, too, such as one describing a motorcycle accident he suffered: "Smallest Cop on Force Laid Up for Repairs."

And one describing a scuffle with intoxicated drivers: "Smallest Cop, Making Arrest, Jails 2 out of 3."

And my favorite: "Smallest of City's Cops Arrests 4 at Once."

I was stunned enough to find that a mental picture I had carried of my grandfather for a half-century was about as skewed as it could be. What was most interesting was to realize how greatly he had benefited from being a small man. It lent an intrigue to his life and magnified his achievements in the eyes of others, who were impressed with what he was able to accomplish in spite of this apparent limitation. The media loved him, and Washingtonians loved reading about him.

My grandfather clearly had certain character traits that helped him. He was a brave man, determined to prove himself, willing to take on challenges from which others twice his size would have shied away. But, especially important, he didn't carry a chip on his shoulder about his size. He was clearly comfortable with it and saw it as a positive factor in his life. It's evident in how people treated him that he had the sort of healthy self-esteem that wins others' affection. His colleagues not only promoted him to assistant chief, but elected him president of the Washington Police Association.

What emerges from the scrapbook is the picture of a man who throughout much of his adult life benefited greatly from a factor that many men would consider a deficit. I'm sensitive to how height can affect self-esteem, measuring in myself at 5 feet 6-½ inches (don't forget the one-half inch). Like my granddad, I've long come to view my stature as a benefit and am grateful for it. Yet walking through life in this particular shell has made me conscious of how it can affect you when you're more often looking up at others than looking down. Many smaller men feel inferior about their size, and some feel that life has dealt them a substantial blow. One young man remarked to me in all honesty that, when he gets to heaven, the first thing he's going to do is ask the Lord why he made him "so blasted short."

It was so refreshing to discover that an ancestor of mine—a respected patriarch in our family—had drawn such advantages from this feature, perfecting self-acceptance of it to an art form. What's most inspiring is that he turned a potential limitation into a major strength.

Keeping Our Limitations in Perspective

Our tendency as humans is to do the opposite—to berate ourselves for our limitations, and to dwell on them to the point that they truly do hinder our success. We desperately need examples like Shorty

Smith's, which by their inspiration and (so often) their comic relief help us to break our fixation on our limitations and to focus on God's bigger picture for our life.

The areas where we may feel life has disadvantaged us are countless, and can include physical features, personality traits, family background, lack of education or experience, shortcomings in our abilities, financial limitations, and endless circumstantial factors that we see as major restrictions.

It may be argued that Milton Smith's short stature wasn't a serious obstacle to him in the way that a major physical disability would have been. Yet physical features we disdain can hinder us greatly because of the effect they have on our self-esteem. We expend vast energy worrying about them, which robs our attention from more important concerns. And, because we imagine they pose limits to our success, we don't try as hard, and our belief becomes a self-fulfilling prophecy. Perceived limitations can restrict us as greatly as genuine ones.

I'm not suggesting we can transcend every limitation and accomplish anything we wish in life. Yet this much is axiomatic: When God wills our success, he almost always works through a combination of strengths and limitations on our part. He uses our strengths to deepen our sense of purpose and partnership with him in his work. He uses them to guide us as well; through understanding our gifts and natural potential, we gain vital insight into his intentions for our life and important directions we should take.

He uses our limitations and weaknesses to strengthen our trust in him, that he will do what we're not capable of accomplishing. He uses them as well to build humility in us, and to increase our sense of adventure in taking steps of faith.

Because of this double dynamic in how God works through us, it's critical that we give far more attention to our strengths than to our limitations in embracing dreams and setting goals. We ought to base our important choices upon what we're most gifted and motivated to do, and only as a secondary matter consider how to meet any challenges our limitations present.

Too often we reverse the process. We focus so greatly on our limitations that we become convinced God has closed doors that he would open for us if we moved forward. We need to make it a matter of lifestyle and daily discipline to shift our attention away from our limitations to the positives—to God's grace and infinite power in our life, and to the gifts he has given us to be productive—much in the way that John Nash learned to focus out his hallucinations in *A Beautiful Mind* and to concentrate on matters that were important in his life's mission. In not a few cases, we find that obstacles we thought were genuine have no more reality than Nash's imaginary friends did.

This manner of thinking is critically important when it comes to the turning-point decisions we're talking about in this book. When a new dream for our life begins to emerge, we're drawn by the conviction that it fits certain strengths and potential we have remarkably well. Yet all too quickly, we begin to dwell on certain limitations we at least imagine we have, which could stand in the way of our success—and we may obsess about them to the point of convincing ourselves we'll fail if we go forward. It's here that thinking positively about our limitations can make a huge difference.

Nine Ways Our Limitations Can Help Us

There is, fortunately, much we can do to change the way we think about our disadvantages and to keep them from having a negative impact upon our destiny. Nothing helps more than if we can turn the tables on a limitation and come to see it as a benefit. We can do this in a surprising number of cases, even to the point of transforming a weakness into a genuine strength.

It helps us to be aware of as many potential benefits of our limitations as possible, and to bring them to mind whenever we're tempted to think life has short-changed us. Our limitations can assist us in at least nine important ways.

1. Others root for us. We see it all the time in sports. People cheer for the underdog. They do *if* the less-advantaged person or team sincerely strives to win; there's no cheering if the underdog takes on a loser mentality and fails to make an earnest effort.

This same dynamic that works for athletes can work for us in areas of life where succeeding means prevailing over an obvious limitation or disadvantage. Others will support us if we give it all our heart.

David benefited greatly from this factor during his period of persecution by Saul. The image of the little guy against the bully carried forward from his fight with Goliath to his effort to stand firm against Saul's oppression yet still serve Israel. People admired how he handled the challenge, loved him dearly and wanted him to succeed. And they *literally* cheered for him: "Saul has slain his thousands, and David his tens of thousands" (1 Sam 18:7).

2. Others are drawn to us. In a similar way, people are attracted to us on a personal level more typically by our weaknesses and limitations than by our strengths. Our inadequacies convey to others that we share a common humanity with them and are not above them.

Timothy, the New Testament pastor, was well-liked by others (Acts 16:2), and Paul himself "wanted Timothy to accompany him" (Acts 16:3 RSV). Timothy was also a shy individual, who had to be exhorted at times not to let his fears discourage him from his mission (1 Tim 4:14, 2 Tim 1:6-7). His shyness seems to have worked well for him in relationships, though, helping others feel he was on their level and approachable.

3. The advantage of lowered expectations—the "in spite of" factor. A particularly interesting benefit of our limitations is how they increase the intrigue people have when we succeed, and their admiration of our accomplishments. In this way, our limitations can actually increase our potential for success.

The members of the Jewish council, for instance, were impressed with how boldly and effectively Peter and John spoke to them about

Jesus in spite of their being "unschooled, ordinary men" (Acts 4:13).

This in-spite-of factor also worked for the woman at the well whom Jesus encountered while traveling by Samaria (John 4). It's evident that her fellow Samaritans thought she was morally loose and disliked her, for she sought water at a well outside the city and in the midday heat—an obvious attempt to avoid contact with people. Following a discussion with Jesus, she returned to Samaria, urging her townspeople, "Come, see a man who told me everything I ever did. Could this be the Messiah?" (Jn 4:29). Their response was so overwhelming that Jesus was inundated with visitors. He felt compelled to stay in the region two more days, and "many of the Samaritans from that town believed in him because of the woman's testimony" (Jn 4:39). Many scholars credit her with being the most effective evangelist in the Gospels, inspiring more conversions to Jesus than any one else did.

What made her testimony so effective was that, because people had such low expectations of her, they listened intently when she suddenly had something important to say. They were astonished she found the courage to speak to them, and that she spoke so persuasively about Jesus being the messiah.

4. Limitations can inspire us to higher achievement. The in-spite-of factor can be a powerful motivator in our own life as well. When we look at what has spurred us to accomplish a goal, we often find that an important part was our desire to prove we could do it in spite of certain disadvantages. In the end, we have to admit that our limitations were a beneficial, if not necessary, factor in finding the heart to succeed.

When Paul stated, "I am the least of the apostles and do not even deserve to be called an apostle," he wasn't espousing false humility but was lamenting that he had persecuted Christians so severely (1 Cor 15:9). Paul was stricken by his past and saw it as a permanent blight upon his life. He could have caved into shame and despair and made no effort to redeem himself. Yet, far to the contrary, he declared, "By the grace of God I am what I am, and his grace to me was not without effect. No, I worked harder than all of them" (1 Cor 15:10). The knowledge of how greatly he had opposed Christ's mission was a potent stimulus to try as hard as he could to reverse the process during his remaining time on earth. What Paul saw as a glaring limitation also gave him extraordinary incentive to do his very best in serving Christ.

5. A limitation becomes a strength. More often than we imagine, it's possible to overcome a limitation completely. The motivation to do so runs so strong that, through determination and focus, and special grace God provides for this effort, we become proficient in an area where we had felt inferior. We may even convert a significant weakness into our greatest strength; no accomplishment is more gratifying.

We see a profound biblical example of such a transformation in Moses' odyssey with public speaking. Moses was so certain he was incapable of effective speaking, and so frightened of trying, that he nearly turned down God's call to deliver Israel. God graciously worked with Moses to wean him of his fears, allowing his brother Aaron to be his spokesman.

Throughout the remainder of Aaron's life, he remained Moses' constant partner in leading Israel. Yet Moses soon was handling many speaking responsibilities himself. We don't find a single reference to his being uncomfortable with the role once he began to gain experience, and he grew competent enough to take over the task completely after Aaron's death (Num 20:23-29). He become such a capable speaker that he moved multitudes with his words, and through his verbal ability lead his people on a massive mission that succeeded against the strongest possible odds. His greatest weakness (or what he perceived as such) became a supremely effective skill.

6. Because we've got it we flaunt it. In some cases, we can do little or nothing to change a limitation; yet by revising the way we think about it, we transform it into a strength. Our physical attractiveness is affected far more by how we feel about our appearance than by any particular characteristic. Simply deciding to esteem a feature we had disliked can make a world of difference in how others see us.

There are many areas of life where choosing to think of a disadvantage as a benefit unleashes our potential considerably. Paul was a master at viewing the most constraining circumstances positively. When he was slammed into prison, he simply assumed it benefited his ministry to be there, and he began looking for how to be most productive (Phil 1:12-14). Some of his most important writing occurred while imprisoned, and it's doubtful this unshakable extrovert would have found the time to write so prolifically and effectively apart from some forced confinement. Whenever we draw help from his epistles today, we're benefiting from the fact that Paul was able to maximize the potential of difficult circumstances so well.

Call this the survivor spirit if you will. It works to our benefit at numerous points.

7. *Polishing the rough edges makes all the difference.* In other cases, a personal feature that has worked against us suddenly starts to benefit us, once we learn to manage it better or modify it. Personality characteristics are often like this. Peter's impulsive temperament frequently got him into trouble during Jesus' earthly ministry. He would speak before thinking—blurting inappropriate statements at the worst times. Yet after Pentecost, this inclination became a strength, for he was able to rise quickly to occasions that required acting immediately without fear of the consequences.

He seized the moment on the day of Pentecost and boldly addressed the curious crowd of diverse nationalities. Others would have seen this challenge as too daunting without careful preparation, missing a golden opportunity present only briefly.

Three years of Jesus' discipling had fine-tuned Peter's instincts, so that he was now able to pick his battles more wisely. With better judgment, his tendency to act on impulse became a positive trait in leading the early church.

8. The empathy factor. Regardless of other benefits it may provide, every limitation has the potential to deepen our empathy for others suffering the same disadvantage. Paul exalts over this point in 2 Corinthians: "Praise be to the God and Father of our Lord Jesus Christ, the Father of compassion and the God of all comfort, who comforts us in all our troubles, so that we can comfort those in any trouble with the comfort we ourselves receive from God" (2 Cor 1:3-4).

Appreciating how God uses our challenges to help us better understand and encourage others who are struggling similarly brings purpose to every trial we experience. We're also able to see benefit to disadvantages that otherwise seem a broadside to our life. Over time, we find they have improved our ability to love others for Christ and have strengthened bonds of friendship.

9. We experience God's grace more fully. Paul suffered a problem—most likely physical—that he termed "a thorn in my flesh." While he never clarified what the "thorn" actually was, it was obviously a major hindrance to him. After Paul prayed earnestly on three occasions for healing, God responded, "my grace is sufficient for you, for my power is made perfect in weakness." Paul then concluded, "when I am weak, then I am strong," suggesting a principle relevant to all believers (2 Cor 12:7-10).

Paul clearly understood that God gives this special strength when we are *genuinely* weak, for he continued praying for healing until God made it plain that he wouldn't remove the thorn. We must always look carefully at whether a weakness or limitation of ours is real and ingrained, or whether it can be healed or transformed into a strength. To the degree we find it's a true disability, we may then count on special compensation from God and a fuller experience of his grace than we would otherwise enjoy.

I've mentioned this point last, even though it's the most important, for unless we consider it in light of the other eight possibilities I've mentioned, we can apply it irresponsibly. We can be too quick to assume God will bless us in spite of a handicap that he'll actually give us the ability to overcome. But when we know that a limitation is permanent, or that a problem absolutely, positively can't be solved, we can then count on an experience of God's grace so exceptional that we'll see our weakness as strength. We'll gain the right to say with Paul, "when I am weak, then I am strong." This is the most revolutionary insight Scripture offers into how a limitation or weakness can work to our advantage.

Great Expectations of Limited Circumstances

Appreciating these many potential advantages of a limitation broadens our thinking and helps us view our life more from the standpoint of faith. We're better able to see how a given limitation of ours may be a benefit to our life as God intends it. His hand in our life is so infinitely creative that there is almost always a positive side to personal challenges that we're missing.

One further point. In revising how we think about our limitations, it's important not only to work on how we view our personal characteristics and the broad circumstances of our life, but the possibilities for each individual day as well.

I made another fascinating discovery about my grandfather while reading his scrapbook. He met his wife Kitty under the most unlikely circumstances. The story is detailed in several news articles, including one titled, "Arrests Girl for Speeding: Weds Her." He stopped Katherine M. Horton for exceeding Washington's speed limit (eighteen mph) as she spun around Dupont Circle. The chance meeting led to a friendship, a relationship, and then marriage.

I was moved (and not a little amused) to discover that my granddad met this remarkable woman through the most routine of police responsibilities—a traffic stop. The story reminds us that God sometimes presents us with unusual opportunities in the midst of mundane daily activities. It speaks to a principle I've longed felt is at the heart of successful living: We ought to begin each day with high expectations for what is ahead, and stay alert to the possibility of God's doing the unexpected. Without the right anticipation, we can miss golden opportunities that so often arise in the form of small beginnings.

I'm impressed with the fact that my grandfather was so alert and seized an outstanding opportunity that unexpectedly arose. It wouldn't have taken much skepticism ("Happy surprises never happen to me, so why expect them?") to blind him to the possibilities in an otherwise annoying situation. I'm equally impressed that he found the courage to pursue a relationship with Kitty, and especially the humility—for it meant swallowing his pride, casting his police authority aside, and admitting that someone he had stopped for breaking the law might be a special gift of God for him.

Something else interesting is that my granddad was widowed at this time. He had married his first wife when they were just teens, but she died tragically at the unlikely age of 26. Grief over such a devastating blow could have kept mind closed to any possibility of marrying again. He was also now the single father of a young boy, and he could have viewed that as hurting his relationship prospects. But he didn't let despair or pessimism blind him to seeing the chance for a fresh start, or keep him from thinking Kitty might be interested in him.

I must say that the more I learn about my grandfather, the more I realize what an amazing man he was. He lived life courageously, and saw it as presenting opportunities where others would see problems. He had an uncanny sense for recognizing a situation's potential, and excellent judgment in taking action. And he was a master at turning disadvantages into strengths.

It all makes me realize I wasn't deluded; that image I had of him as a four-year-old was correct after all.

While he's a giant in my life for good reason, I hope his example inspires you also to see your limitations as strengths, and not to let them deter you from new adventures God has in store for you. I hope he encourages you as well not to let a past loss or failure keep you from seeing the chance to begin again.

Make it your lifestyle to think of your limitations *creatively*.

Consider how they may benefit you, especially when you're pursing a goal or dream that fits you well. Consider the different ways they may help and not hinder your success, and keep these possibilities in the forefront of your mind. Such optimistic reflecting will greatly improve the quality of your daily life, and will help you recognize and seize a great opportunity when it's time for a major life change.

5

Past Guidance and Present Decisions

Jennifer is considering a job offer that seems good from every angle except one: she's uncertain how to reconcile it with a past experience of guidance.

When Jennifer was offered her current job as a legal secretary in Sacramento, she was living in Tallahassee. She was a new Christian then, and eager to be certain about God's will.

On a balmy May afternoon, she spent several hours walking on a Gulf beach, praying for God's guidance. After praying for about an hour, she felt a surge of conviction that God wanted her to accept the offer. This wonderful feeling of assurance stayed with her for another hour or so, as she continued to walk and pray. That period of inspiration was the deciding point for Jennifer, and she resolved to make the move and take the job. She has thought back to that time often while in Sacramento, and taken reassurance that she is where God wants her to be.

Now Jennifer has been offered a new job with a law firm in Denver. She would like to accept the offer. It's a better match for her talents than her present position, and provides a salary boost as well. Jennifer likes the attorney who wants to hire her, and believes she would work comfortably with him.

Yet Jennifer fears she would be disobeying God by leaving Sacramento. Although she has prayed much about it, she hasn't had an experience of inspiration similar to the one in Tallahassee. She *has* seen many practical reasons why she should make this move. She wonders if God may be guiding her through them, and if it's okay to base her decision on these positive factors alone. But the lack of a definite sense of call to take this step is unsettling to her. Is she obliged to stay in Sacramento until God clearly tells her to leave?

A Common Predicament

Many Christians experience a dilemma like Jennifer's. They struggle with how to integrate past guidance from God with new insights they've gained into their potential, interests and emerging opportunities. Are they locked in to their past understanding of God's will? Does it present a binding call upon them? Or are they free to consider a new direction for their life?

Some, like Jennifer, have had an episode of past guidance dramatic enough that they wonder if they must stay committed to it until God clearly tells them to change course. Many others, who cannot recall a specific experience of guidance, still have lived with an understanding of God's will for their life for so long that they feel uneasy considering any other alternatives.

I've known more than a few Christians who, when they were young—in junior or senior high, or even earlier—grew convinced God wanted them to devote their life to a certain career, yet in college found this option wasn't a good match for them. Discovering a disparity between what they believe God wills for them and what is realistic for them educationally is shattering to the idealism of some Christian students. Even harder for some is finding their own interests have changed, and that they're now attracted to a different vocational dream than the one they've long assumed was God's will.

I have personally gone through two periods of career reassessment where I had difficulty letting go of a past understanding of God's will. I mentioned earlier that I grappled for about a year with whether to shift from a music career to teaching. I finally decided to switch, and as a start, enrolled in the doctor of ministry program at Fuller Theological Seminary. My intent was to study how God guides our personal decisions, to better prepare to teach and write on the subject. But after a year at Fuller, I decided to try church ministry, thinking I might best use my teaching gifts there. I accepted a call to a church in St. Louis. But while there, I found myself dreaming often about launching an independent teaching ministry. I wrestled with making that change also for about a year. In both cases, I had grown so accustomed to a particular identity—first as a musician, then as a pastor—that I feared I might violate God's will by taking a new direction.

One thing that complicated my decision to leave church ministry was that a pastor I respected had sincerely told me he believed I was also ordained to that vocation. I esteemed him so highly that his advice seemed a divine oracle. I knew he merely meant to be encouraging and not pontifical. Still, his pronouncement became a hurdle I had to jump in deciding to shift from pastoring to the independent ministry I finally formed.

Binding Calls and Unfolding Calls

Christians who find it hard to reconcile past guidance with a new direction that seems right for them usually respond in one of several ways. Some feel compelled to wait for God to give them further guidance so convincing that they'll have no doubt he wants them to make the change. Others move ahead without such guidance, but experience plenty of guilt as they do.

Still others are spurred to re-examine their basic assumptions about guidance, to see whether these have been realistic. Some discover that they've been operating with unreasonable ideas about how God guides—which have led them to read too much into past experiences of guidance, and to expect too much guidance for present decisions. This reassessment is liberating for them, for they realize God is giving them greater freedom to take new directions than they had assumed.

When Christians like Jennifer find that a step which now seems best for their life seems to conflict with past guidance from God, they often are thinking of guidance as a static process. They're assuming God reveals his will for some area of our life once and for all, and that's it; we're then locked in to that understanding for a long time, perhaps permanently.

Scripture, though, pictures God's guidance as a *dynamic* process. He seldom reveals much about his will for our future, but lets us discover it step by step as we move along. And purely practical insights we gain into ourselves and our opportunities are often as important in understanding his will as our more dramatic experiences of guidance. While God can give us a binding, non-negotiable call to do something, his calls—to vocations especially—are more often *unfolding,* and best understood only as we're in motion. Appreciating this aspect of how God guides helps us greatly in understanding the relationship of past guidance to present decisions.

Paul's Apostolic Call—the Exception or the Rule?

Scripture does show instances of God's mandating someone to follow a vocation permanently, as a life commitment. The most familiar example, for most of us, is God's calling Paul to be an apostle. Paul begins most of his letters with a reference to this call, declaring that he is "called to be an apostle," or is "an apostle by the will of God" (Acts 1:1, 5; 1 Cor 1:1; 2 Cor 1:1; Gal 1:1; Eph 1:1; Col 1:1; 1 Tim 1:1; 2 Tim 1:1; Tit 1:1-3). He clearly understood this role as an indelible stamp from God upon his life. Most likely, he received this commission by direct revelation from God during his Damascus Road episode.

Many Christians assume Paul's apostolic call is a model for how they should personally expect to receive God's guidance. They believe that if they're spiritually mature enough and alert to God, he will give them a call to follow a certain career that's as clear and distinct as he gave Paul. He will then expect them to stay on this course until further notice, even for life. This same assumption leads many to believe they've actually received such a call if, like Jennifer, they've had a dramatic or unusual experience of guidance.

Paul, however, never claimed that his experience of being called was normative for other Christians. Nowhere in his writings does he teach that anyone should expect such dramatic, explicit guidance in career decisions, nor do we find him anywhere counseling someone to seek this level of guidance. Rather, he encouraged Christians, in discerning God's will for their lives, to consider practical factors—such as their gifts, the opportunities open to them and the counsel of other people.

Paul's Typical Experience with Guidance
But how would Paul counsel someone like Jennifer, who believes she has been called by God to be where she is, but now sees compelling reasons to take a new direction with her life? I believe we find an important clue in an episode from Paul's life described in Acts 16:8-40. It begins with Paul receiving guidance from God dramatic enough that he regards it as a call. Yet at several points he responds to this call differently than he did to the one to be an apostle, even revising his understanding of it as he moves ahead.

One night, Luke (the writer of Acts) tells us, "Paul had a vision of a man of Macedonia standing and begging him, 'Come over to Macedonia and help us.' After Paul had seen the vision, we got ready at once to leave for Macedonia, concluding that God had called us to preach the gospel to them" (vv. 9-10).

Paul has a vision—possibly a dream—of a man in Macedonia pleading for his help. Paul and his companions take this incident as a revelation, concluding that God is calling them to go to Macedonia and evangelize. Interestingly, this is the only occasion in the New Testament, outside of references to Paul's apostolic commission, where he is described as being called by God to do something.

We would logically assume, since Paul received such exceptional guidance to go to Macedonia, that his experience once he arrives will parallel his vision exactly: he'll find a man ministering there who is desperate for his aid, and then devote himself to helping this man evangelize the Macedonians. We look in vain, however, throughout the detailed description of Paul's visit to Macedonia in Acts 16, for any reference to this man.

Instead, soon after arriving in Macedonia, Paul and his party encounter a group of women praying by a river, and one remarkable woman, Lydia, leading them. Paul persuades Lydia to become a Christian. She then convinces Paul and his team to stay at her home. The fact that they accept Lydia's offer is good evidence that Paul has concluded he isn't going to find the man of his vision, for otherwise he probably would be holding out for the opportunity to lodge with him.

Paul, then, makes a significant revision of his call, and decides to minister with Lydia and develop a church based in her home. What's most interesting is that, while Paul's initial guidance to go to Macedonia came through a supernatural vision, his change of direction resulted from practical insights—his discovery that Lydia and her friends were available for ministry, and that the man of his vision, apparently, wasn't to be found. Paul seemed to place as much weight on such practical factors in understanding God's will as he did upon direct revelation!

One other logical assumption we might make is that, since Paul was led to Macedonia by a vision, he would be obliged to stay there indefinitely—at least until God gave him equally dramatic guidance to leave. Yet after a tumultuous episode with some Macedonian businessmen, who fear Paul's ministry is hurting them financially, the town officials ask Paul to leave—and he agrees. In all, Paul stays in Macedonia probably only several months. And his decision to move on is based not on further dramatic guidance, but on purely practical considerations.

God's Guidance through Our Filters

From Paul's Macedonian call, then, we learn several vital lessons about God's guidance. First, the fact that we might receive dramatic or supernatural guidance doesn't necessarily mean we will fully understand its content. Nor does it mean that God has necessarily spoken his final word to us on a matter. Some revising of our understanding may be needed as we move ahead. We interpret God's guidance, like anything else, through our filters; we may grasp some parts of it correctly, but misunderstand others, and need to rethink our conclusions as he enlightens us further.

I suspect, too, that Paul's Macedonian vision—as is typical with dreams—was at least partly symbolic. God may have intended it more as inspiration to get him moving in the right direction, than as a revelation of exact events that would take place. We shouldn't discount the possibility that an inspiration or epiphany we experience is more symbolic than factual. It may be God's means of moving us forward, yet not a precise revelation of what will take place, or of what will be required of us. Our future will still take many twists and turns that aren't apparent yet, and we will need to look to God often for fresh guidance about what to do.

Paul's experience also teaches us an important lesson about the role of practical thinking in guidance, and its interplay with more dramatic experiences of guidance we might have. While God may direct us on occasion through supernatural guidance, he more typically reveals the details of his will for our lives through practical information. He has given us a mind and expects us to use it! Logical conclusions we reach, through observing the circumstances of life, can be at least as important in understanding God's will as the insight that comes through exceptional guidance. And while God may lead us to take an important step with our life through a special call, he may also expect us, through practical insight, to modify our understanding of the call as we move forward.

Paul's experience also demonstrates that God's calls can have their time limits. In the case of Paul's visit to Macedonia, the period was fairly brief. This suggests that even if God gives us a dramatic call to do something, the time may come when he expects us to make a practical decision to change directions. While he can then give us a special call to move on, it's just as likely he'll expect us to simply use good judgment in making this choice.

Reaching the Right Conclusions

Paul's call to go to Macedonia, then, differed significantly from his apostolic call. When God called Paul to become an apostle, it appears God told him once and for all that he was to fulfill this role for life. This call conferred a permanent status on Paul. Paul's Macedonian call, on the other hand, was less precise, and served mainly to propel him ahead. Only as he moved forward, did the nature of his responsibility in Macedonia become clear, along with the time commitment involved.

Scripture, then, pictures two types of calls God bestows on Christians—the one clear and binding, the other unfolding.

But how should we determine whether guidance we receive is meant to place a binding call on us, or is part of an unfolding one? The answer, I believe, has to do with the clarity and intensity of the guidance. Paul's call to apostleship likely came through his Damascus Road experience. On Damascus Road and in the days following, Paul heard God's audible voice clearly and distinctly. Paul had no question about who was speaking to him, or about the details of what God was instructing him to do. Moreover, the event was remarkably intense, leaving Paul blinded for several days. God also provided confirmation of his guidance, and further instruction, through Ananias, whom he commissioned to heal Paul of his blindness and counsel him.

Paul's Macedonian vision, on the other hand, was a much briefer, less intense event. The guidance it conveyed was also less clear than that on Damascus Road, and there's no indication Paul heard God speaking audibly. Luke notes that after Paul had the vision, those in his party concluded that God had called them to preach the gospel in Macedonia. The fact that they reached a conclusion about what to do indicates they discussed Paul's vision and its implications; the vision required some *interpretation*, in other words.

For most of us, even our most dramatic episodes of guidance are usually more similar to Paul's Macedonian vision than to his Damascus Road experience. If that. While we may occasionally have a dream so unusual that it seems like a direct revelation from God, our guidance occasions are more typically like Jennifer's on the beach. We have an inspiration—a "Eureka-I've-found-it" moment of insight into what to do. Yet we haven't heard God's audible voice, or experienced some other lucid revelation of guidance. We've merely had an *impression* of what God wants us to do.

God may be giving us important guidance through this impression, to be sure. Still, it's an impression, coming through our own sensors, and subject to all the human factors that can skew our understanding. It's always a safe rule of thumb in such cases to assume that our grasp of God's will is partial at best, and will need some revision as we move forward.

We should expect that if God gives us a binding call, his guidance will be so distinct and emphatic that we'll have no doubt he has spoken, and no question about what he's telling us to do. Less intense experiences of guidance, such as a moment of inspiration or a dream, should be regarded as part of an unfolding call. They are part of the enlightenment God is using to steer us in the right direction. Yet we will still need plenty of further guidance as we put our feet in motion.

Staying Flexible and Staying Faithful

Nothing we're saying about the importance of staying flexible with respect to guidance, however, gives us a license to break commitments to others or to be flighty. Anytime we choose to take a fresh direction with our life, we need to give our new situation a fair chance before changing course again. And we should always consider carefully if we've made commitments to others—explicit or implicit—that should be fulfilled before we allow ourselves permission to move on.

Some vocational roles require you to promise to serve in them for a specific period of time. These include many missionary and ministry positions, where others may be depending heavily upon you to keep your commitment. If you have made such a pledge of service, you should only consider leaving early under the most compelling circumstances (we'll look at what these might be in the appendix section, "Promises and Vows"), or if those who've employed you are willing to release you.

Yet even when we've given a situation a fair chance, and wouldn't be violating commitments by moving on, we may still wonder if we must remain bound to a past understanding of God's will. Appreciating how God gives unfolding calls can keep us from restricting ourselves unnecessarily in such a case.

Jennifer, for instance, has certainly given her job in Sacramento a reasonable commitment of time, and isn't being unfaithful in considering a change. I believe Paul would counsel her to take the job in Denver. He would tell her that the guidance she received to move to Sacramento was important. Yet it wasn't meant to lock her in forever, nor was it God's final word on her career. Moving to Sacramento was necessary, in fact, for her to be in a position to then receive the offer from Denver, and to be able to understand why this new opportunity is now right for her.

I believe that Paul would counsel any of us who are in a situation similar to Jennifer's to be flexible and open to the possibility God has new horizons for us. Paul himself showed remarkable flexibility in his odyssey described in Acts 16.

His example demonstrates, too, that it's God's nature to bring new adventures into our lives. During our lifetime, he gives us many fresh experiences and challenges, to stimulate us to grow and to realize our potential for Christ. A certain desire for adventure is essential if we're to be alert and open to the best opportunities God presents us.

We can have too much wanderlust, to be sure. We can yearn for fresh experience so much that we have difficulty keeping commitments, and fail to enjoy the simple routines of life.

Yet the opposite danger is equally real—that we don't desire adventure enough, become too stuck in the inertia of life, and resist change. Paul, I believe, demonstrates a healthy balance in the extensive picture of his life in the New Testament. He longed to grow and to experience all the new vistas God had for him. Yet he was equally determined to be faithful to his commitments, and to find joy in life's ordinary pleasures.

We should pray that God gives us this same balance in our own outlook. It will keep us pliable and open to his best, as his plan for our life unfolds.

6

Regretting the Choice That Seemed So Right
(When Is a Decision Truly a Bad One?)

We've stressed that God's guidance is an unfolding process
for each of us. Our grasp of his will in any matter comes not in one
overwhelming epiphany, but step by step as we stay in motion. And
we've noted two ways that this understanding helps us. It frees us
to take a new direction with our life, even though our knowledge of
the future and of God's will is less than complete. And it keeps us
from thinking we're mandated to stay in a situation that no longer
fits us well, just because originally we had been strongly confident
of God's guidance to be there.

Appreciating the step-by-step nature of God's guidance can also
help us in another way, which I want to look at in this chapter. We
may conclude that a past decision, which seemed right at the time,
was actually misguided—and now we despair over the implications.

We missed God's will in that choice, we assume. That belief can lead us to fear we've forever forsaken the chance to enjoy his perfect plan for our future. The fear that we're no longer in-line with God's perfect plan can discourage us from seeking new direction from him, and from taking new steps of faith. Despair over a past decision we believe was mistaken can shut us down, destroy our optimism and keep us from thinking creatively about our future.

Understanding the unfolding manner of God's guidance can make a world of difference in such a case, as we'll note. But first, let's look at how regret over a past decision can develop, and the slippery slope that can result.

When Hindsight Is 20/20
When Chandra was 39, she left a lucrative job in banking to pursue a counseling career. Long wanting to make this change, she chose to move forward when a psychologist friend promised her a position with his counseling firm once she completed the necessary training. Spurred on by his gracious offer of employment, she enrolled in a masters program full time, living off savings till she finished her studies.

Chandra's friend indeed hired her once she graduated. But a short time later he left the practice due to health issues. Without his leadership, the center foundered, other counselors resigned, and it folded within a year.

Chandra lacked the clients and momentum to launch an independent practice, and she was unable to find work with another counseling agency in the Boston area where she lived. With her savings now depleted, she returned to a banking job, leaving her counseling dream on indefinite hold.

When Chandra shared her experience with me, she said she was certain God had taught her a lesson through these frustrating circumstances. He had shown her that she missed his will in attempting to become a counselor. She spoke repeatedly of having made a "bad decision." As I probed a bit, it became clear that her ruminating wasn't just ventilation or an exercise in self-pity. She was strongly convinced she had made an unfortunate mistake, and she had never questioned this assumption since the doors at the counseling center closed several years before. The conviction she had failed greatly increased her discouragement, and dampened her zeal to risk a dream again.

Chandra was understandably surprised when I shared my own observation. I felt that her decision to enter the counseling profession hadn't been a bad one at all, and that she shouldn't be worrying about having missed God's will. She had based her choice on the best information she had at the time—that she had obvious talent and long-standing motivation to become a counselor, plus an exceptional offer of employment. And she was taking a step that would increase her potential to contribute meaningfully to the needs of others. Especially important, she was a serious Christian who earnestly wanted God's will, and she had prayed seriously about her decision.

Which of us, I thought, faced with her circumstances, would have decided differently?

Of course, had Chandra *known* how events would transpire, she never would have left banking for counseling. But that's exactly the point. God seldom tips his hand about our future, and he guides us as much by information he withholds from us as by information he gives.

Let me repeat that point: *God guides us as much by information he withholds from us as by information he gives.*

He allows us to develop dreams and expectations, and he uses them to move us ahead. In some cases, he fulfills a dream moreless as we envision it. In other cases, his intent isn't to fulfill it but to use it to draw us to a point where, with the new insight we've gained, we can now see clearly to take a new direction. Through the whole process, he nurtures us with experiences of growth that never would have been ours if we had known the future—for then we never would have taken our venture of faith. But the education we gain through life's unexpectedly bumpy paths is critical to our development, and God integrates it into our further experience in remarkable ways.

I obviously don't know God's intentions for Chandra's future. Whatever she does, I'm certain God will use her training and her experiences at the counseling center in ways that enhance her ministry for Christ and are deeply gratifying to her—if she stays open to him and pliable.

This is the lesson from the experience of another friend of mine who, some years ago, left the computer field to become a pastor. Though his congregations loved him, denominational issues made it difficult for him to minister in a church position. Finally, he left church ministry and, with some chagrin, took a job with a computer manufacturing firm once again. Yet he was soon granted permission to hold a weekly Bible study at that company, which many began attending. His pastoral background opened doors for ministry at that firm that would have been closed to him before. His is an inspiring example of how God uses the total mix of experiences in our life—the successes and the disappointments—to make us each uniquely effective.

Broken Dreams

When a dream that we follow backfires, it's only human to question our original decision to pursue it, and to wonder if our mind was on vacation then. Many are unduly hard on themselves—even if they had based their choice on the best information they possibly could have had, and the circumstances that derailed their dream were impossible to foresee. We Christians are more prone to berate ourselves than anyone at such a time. Not only do we question our past judgment, but we get caught up in torturous questions about God's will. The fact that we encounter any problems at all in a new venture can make us fear we've missed God's will, and that concern deepens our sense of failure.

Dealing with failed expectations is difficult enough. Any of us who has suffered a setback as crushing as Chandra's needs time to grieve our loss and to work through our feelings of disappointment. Yet add to this the conviction that our original decision was unsound, and our regret can be overwhelming. It can make us doubt that we have the competence now to turn our life around. And the guilt we feel over missing God's will can keep us locked in place, fearing we lack the potential to follow his guidance successfully, and that our future options are now forever less ideal.

We should make a keen effort at such a time to imagine ourselves back in the context in which we made our first choice. What were our circumstances then? What were the facts as we knew them? Were we open to God's will? Did we make a reasonable effort to seek it? If, in fact, our decision was the best it could have been under the circumstances, we should be gentle and affirming with ourselves now. We should strive to think as positively as we possibly can about that past decision. Rather than assume it was bungled, we should regard it as a wise, competent choice—which in time may even prove to have been brilliant and enlightened.

We should strive also to appreciate the dynamic nature of God's guidance, and how he brings us to important points in our life's journey most often by a circuitous route. In time, we'll likely look back on our current crisis as a vital turning point, which God has used to open up welcome new horizons for us. Such faith-inspired thinking will help us greatly to break the spell of regret, and to better recognize God's new directions for us now.

Taking Heart at Turning Points
This isn't to say we're incapable of making bad decisions as Christians. We find many examples in Scripture where an otherwise godly person is shown displaying bad judgment. But in every case, that person was either insensitive to God's leading, untrusting of him or unfaithful to him—and in a major way. The leaders of Israel were beguiled into making a treaty of peace with Gibeon, for instance, because they "did not ask direction from the Lord" (Jos 9:14 RSV).

I'm not aware of any instance in Scripture, however, where someone made a reasonable effort to understand God's will and make a decision responsibly, and yet the biblical writer judged that choice incompetent because of the results. Individuals themselves often questioned the sanity of decisions that God in fact had led them to make. Moses was so exasperated at Pharaoh's initial refusal to allow the Jews to leave Egypt that he thought he had made the mistake of his life in petitioning the ruler to let them go. And when the Israelites faced challenges in their desert march, they concluded they had erred horribly in leaving Egypt, even though they were initially ecstatic to break free of slavery there.

Yet never do we find a biblical writer passing judgment on someone's good-faith decision due to problems that arose. The obstacles people encountered in such cases always have a higher purpose. Sometimes God used these setbacks to strengthen their faith, their trust in him and their resolve to stay committed to a challenging course of action. This was clearly his intent with all the difficulties the Israelites endured en route to Canaan, which never on any occasion were an indictment on their original decision to leave Egypt.

In other cases, God used hindrances to signal that, however enlightened someone's initial decision was, he or she should now take a new direction. We see various instances of God's guiding in this manner in Acts 16. Paul is twice hindered from entering regions where he wants to minister—Asia and Bithynia—then ends up in Troas briefly, only to be redirected to Macedonia (vv 6-10). We looked at Paul's trip to Macedonia in the last chapter, noting how he had to change direction once there significantly several times (vv 11-40).

Any time you or I take a step of faith but then encounter a significant setback, we face the task of determining God's intent. Is he merely testing our faith, and not wanting this problem to deter us from forging ahead toward our goal? Or is he showing us that we should now take a fresh direction? Discerning God's will in such a case can be no small challenge. Being confident our original decision was sound doesn't relieve us of the need now to pray earnestly and to draw once again on everything we know about how God guides.

But how we think about that decision can radically affect our ability to understand God now, since concern about it can weigh us down to the point of distraction. Fortunately, we may be freed forever from the fear that we might now have to regard a past choice that we made responsibly as misguided. That we're not compelled to have second thoughts about it is tremendously liberating in itself. It can save us from the downward spiral of regret, and allow us the mental energy to confront our current situation creatively and optimistically. This is enormously good news for any of us who are inclined to comb over our past and to condemn ourselves for what we cannot change.

How Badly Can We Miss God's Will?

An issue remains, and it can be a thorny one. The perspective we're suggesting on past choices is reassuring *if* we know we were open to God's will in a given decision and did our best to make it responsibly. But what if the opposite was true? We rushed our decision, without regard to what God wanted. Or we failed to trust him adequately, and followed the course of least resistance, instead of taking on challenges that would have been healthy for us. Or we knew full well that God wanted us to take a certain path, but in disobedience chose another.

And what if the decision in question was a pivotal one, which forever affects our life in a significant way? Have we irrevocably missed God's perfect will for the rest of our days? Are we compelled now to live with his second best?

Some well-meaning Christians will answer that, yes, God's second best is all we can settle for now. I once read a popular book on knowing God's will in which the author spoke with regret about an early vocational decision. God had called him to missionary service when he was young, he explained, but he chose instead to become a physician. Now, writing much later in life, he lamented that he had forever removed himself from God's perfect plan by following a medical career, and was only in position now to experience God's second-best options.

The author's humility in speaking so freely of his own failure was refreshing. Yet his view of God was tragically small. Would the all-powerful God whom he served, who loved him so greatly, really let him get away with a mistake of this dimension?

Abraham failed profoundly in seeking to have a child by Hagar, and he and his family suffered consequences thereafter. Yet his sin didn't deter God from bringing about the most important aspects of his plan for Abraham: Sarah still bore a child in her old age, and Abraham still became the father of countless descendants.

David sinned even more greatly when he sought a tryst with Bathsheba, and then had her husband killed in war. The consequences in this case were especially severe: God slew Bathsheba's son whom she bore by David, in spite of David's earnest pleas that God would spare the child. That punishment, plus rebuke from the prophet Nathan, drove David to sincere repentance and deep sorrow over his lapse. But Scripture never implies that, from this point on, David had to live with God's second best for his life. God still fulfilled his major promises for David. Most interestingly, God even worked David's most serious mistake into his plan. Bathsheba became his wife, and it was she who gave birth to Solomon, the son who succeeded David on the throne. "She gave birth to a son, and they named him Solomon. The LORD loved him" (2 Sam 12:24).

At first, it seems surprising that God allowed Bathsheba to have this supremely positive role in David's life. Wasn't God being overly permissive here? And wasn't David left thinking he had benefited from his sin, and from now on could presume upon God's grace? I suspect, though, that the effect upon David was quite the opposite. God's action undoubtedly was deeply humbling to him—an extraordinary reminder of just how thoroughly God was in control of his destiny.

This unspeakably far-reaching role that God plays in our lives as believers is best described by Paul, when he notes that God chose us to follow Christ "before the creation of the world" (Eph 1:4). This means that our sin doesn't take him by surprise, and doesn't fatally broadside his plan for our life. He knows when and how we'll fail before we ever do. He makes no promise to protect us from the unfortunate results of our sin. But when we sincerely repent and seek his forgiveness, *we put ourselves in position to enjoy his best for our life from that point forward.* To say we have forever removed ourselves from God's perfect will in this case is to paint too small a picture of God, and to miss the authority he takes for working out his plan for us.

When we know we have truly failed Christ, repentance is exceedingly important, and we should focus intently on seeking forgiveness. Yet, as time moves on, he doesn't wish us to be sidelined with regret, but wants us to focus on the future, not the past—and to take heart that he will work even our most heinous failures into his perfect plan for our life.

Don't Look Back
Indeed, God wants us to be *much* more focused on the future than the past. Faith in Christ generates hope and optimism about our future; we may assume that abiding regret about the past isn't inspired by him. Dwelling on our past is a bottomless pit; in some cases we simply don't know what our motives were in a certain bygone decision. We may not even remember clearly what our mental state was then, and we have no way of knowing if that choice was truly in God's will. Yet it makes no difference now; we can still enjoy God's very best options for our future if we stay open to him and pliable.

And so we have enormous incentive to continue to dream big and think creatively about our future. Even if we've seriously erred in the past, God graciously extends to us the chance to start over. We must not allow guilt, regret or shame over our past to restrict our ability to embrace a vibrant new vision for our life.

If we can let go of obsession with our past, we've won a major victory toward envisioning our future. We position ourselves to grasp God's best new options for us and lock in to them. We can turn our focus instead to another battle, which is also substantial for many of us: conquering our fears and apprehensions about what's ahead. In the next section, we'll examine how a number of concerns about the future—ranging from fears of failure to fears of success—can keep us from pursuing a promising new direction. And we'll look at how we can get the upper hand on our fears, and gain the courage for life's most important steps of faith.

The challenge of mastering our fears is fortunately achievable for each of us, and so you'll find much reason for hope in the pages ahead.

Part Two

Finding the Courage
To Reinvent Yourself

7

The Fear of Failure

For some time I'd been struggling to ride a two-wheel bike *without training wheels, but with no success. I kept repeating the same ritual—pedaling a few yards until the bicycle began to tilt, then putting my foot out to break the fall. My problem wasn't inability but lack of confidence. A bike has to be moving at more than a snail's pace to stay upright. But I was frightened to pedal fast enough to give it the needed thrust, afraid I'd wipe out severely.*

My dad was convinced I would learn to balance, and kept reassuring me. His confidence gave me the hope to try and try again. With his help, I was able to enjoy the fantasy of conquering the two-wheeler for brief periods of time. Dad would hold on to the bike's seat and run alongside while I pedaled furiously. We'd make good headway for a block or two until he got winded. I was adamant about one thing, though: he wasn't to take his hand off the seat. I kept reminding him again and again.

One day he decided to trust his own judgment. After ambling through several hilly blocks, we came to a level stretch entering a new development next to our neighborhood. I began pedaling hard and picked up a head of steam. The momentum felt great, and I turned my head to smile at dad. Only then did I realize that he hadn't been holding the bike at all, but was standing with arms folded a block back, grinning from ear to ear. I had accomplished my first solo bike ride without knowing it!

My victory with the two-wheeler came for a single reason: my father believed in me more than I believed in myself. He kept encouraging me to try, then took his hand off the bike at just the right moment, so I'd discover for myself that I could do it. He believed in me to the point that I succeeded.

I share this story from *Reach Beyond Your Grasp* because it's my earliest memory of being seriously stymied by the fear of failure.[1] I didn't simply fear toppling over if I attempted to bike solo— I was *certain* I would, and so convinced that I couldn't risk trying. My fear of failing was so severe that, without my dad's creative tactic, I wouldn't likely have attempted a solo ride any time soon.

The fear of failing pervaded my life as a child, adolescent and early teenager, and held me back in many ways. It took another breakthrough experience to show me just how exaggerated my fears really were.

Early in eighth grade I fell for a girl in my class. Yet, painfully shy, I couldn't muster the courage to ask her out. For months I tried to do it, and spent many evenings by the phone, dialing her number but then hanging up before the first ring occurred. I suffered the most hideous fears—that she would tease me, laugh at me, belittle me if I asked her for a date. Even the possibility of a polite no was mortifying.

Finally one evening in February, an older friend at my side encouraging me on, I dialed her number, and the first ring occurred before I could hang up. I hung on for dear life, and her dad answered. Terrified, I asked to speak to her. She was quickly on the phone and . . . was thrilled to hear from me. I could scarcely believe it. She eagerly accepted when I asked her to the movies for that

Saturday night. Best of all, a dating relationship resulted that lasted over a year, and greatly enriched our lives as young teenagers.

These two experiences, from my early childhood and early teenage years, helped teach me how stunningly illusive the fear of failure can be. In each I was on the verge of a major breakthrough, and yet was so frightened of failing that I couldn't go ahead. Without someone else's strong support in each case, I probably would have stayed stuck in my fears.

Discovering firsthand the deceptive nature of the fear of failure is one of the most important growth experiences any of us can have. Most of us have in our memory bank a store of happy episodes while growing up, like these I've just mentioned, which helped us recognize how wide our fears can hit of the mark of reality. In the best case, these experiences have propelled us to take greater risks as adults, and to enjoy greater rewards.

Yet self-consistency is a powerful force, as we've noted, and most of us have to often relearn this lesson about how easily the fear of failure deceives us. Taking a new venture usually requires dealing with certain fears of failing, which too often leave us far too risk-adverse.

The fear that we'll fail so often distorts our view of reality horribly, and prevents us from pursuing dreams we can actually achieve. Among the many factors that hold us back from important new horizons, none is more effective than the fear of failing. Or insidious. Our conviction we'll fail can grow so strong that we not only feel justified staying immobile, but believe we're being responsible. Yet far too often that belief is as mistaken as my assumptions of disaster were as a young child about biking solo, or as a young teenager about asking my classmate out.

When Fearing Failure Is Healthy

This isn't to say the fear of failure is always unhealthy. *Some* fear of failing is usually helpful, and necessary to our success. The benefits of fearing failure can be seen most obviously in the case of unhealthy or dangerous behavior.

Late-night comedian Johnny Carson, for instance—to cite just one of countless examples—knew chronic smoking could damage your health, but believed he was personally invincible. Yet emphysema plagued his later years, and he died at 79, probably prematurely. A greater fear of the consequences of smoking would have served him well as a young man. To say it differently, a greater fear that smoking would fail to deliver long-term happiness would likely have left his later years much happier.

Similarly for a dear friend of mine, who for many years has suffered from hepatitis C and other health problems, stemming from years of serious drug and alcohol abuse. A greater fear that his indulgences would lead to misery would have benefited him greatly.

If reckless behavior doesn't injure or kill us, it will likely diminish our happiness over the long term. Here bland optimism is our worst enemy. We each need a strong fear of failure whenever we're tempted to imagine risky behavior might improve our life.

In the same way, we may entertain a dream or goal which, while right for someone else, is a poor fit for us. Each of us, for instance, from time to time cherishes the fantasy of mastering a certain skill that's either outside of our range of potential, or isn't a wise investment of our time. In these cases fearing failure saves us from a lot of disappointment.

A man I know has longed for ages to become a successful pop singer fronting a band. The problem is that he can't match pitch well, lacks an appealing voice, has poor stage presence, and doesn't work well with others (did I cover everything?). And yet, bound and determined to make his fantasy a reality, he has made himself a pest within the music community where he lives, trying to interest others in helping him, and is a burden to those running open mics. He seems to harbor no fear of failure at all, which would truly help him.

His example is extreme, to be sure. But it does demonstrate how we can get into a rut pursuing a dream that doesn't work well for us. Please understand that I err strongly on the side of encouraging people to pursue their dreams, especially artistic ones. But each of us has only so much time to work with in life, and we do best to invest it in ways that match both our desires and our natural potential. In cases like this man's, the solution can be to look for a different way to fulfill a creative passion, which matches our inherent potential better. He doesn't need to let go of his love for music, for instance, and his longing to be "part of the show." But there are many other ways he can serve a band and be part of the music community without being a star performer. Possibilities could be managing or booking a band, running sound or helping with equipment. He should look for a role that fits his talent better, yet still gives some expression to his artistic dream.

I went down a wrong track with a different sort of creative dream, when I was about 30. I began to long to be skilled at auto repair and to handle my own maintenance. Some of my male friends took pride in doing so, and it seemed manly to follow their example. And so I bought a b0ook on car repair and studied it carefully. Finally, the chance came to act on my erudition, and a friend agreed to help me replace my station wagon's alternator. We labored almost a full day on the project, which would have taken a professional mechanic just minutes. Even then, I was less than confident we had done everything correctly.

After that day, reality sunk in. I had blown my one day off that week on a project that was less fun than I had entertained, and so the recreational value had been minimal. More important, time is precious. It didn't seem a wise investment of time to handle my own auto repair, since I was more gifted and motivated to fill other roles. The hours spent tinkering with my car could be better invested in writing, counseling or preparing a talk, while a professional fixes my car—and more capably than I could hope to do. I began to fear that further attempts of mine at this DIY maintenance would be less than competent—and in this case the fear of failure was my ally.

Fearing Failure Enough to Prepare Well

In addition to keeping us from certain primrose paths, the fear of failure can benefit us in another important way. Some fear of failing motivates us to prepare well for a venture that's truly right for us, and in right measure this anxiety is essential to our success. The better we're able to peer into the future and identify potential problems we may encounter, and then take steps to prevent them or endure them, the more likely we are to succeed. Here, a healthy dose of negative thinking serves us well. We need to fear the possibility of these obstacles enough to be ready to meet them successfully. And we need to fear the possibility of certain consequences enough to avoid being careless.

I'm certain vastly more people fail because they don't prepare sufficiently for certain challenges than because the dream they're pursuing doesn't fit them well. Consider the large number of small businesses that fold each year because they are undercapitalized. A new enterprise may be fundamentally a good idea, which will succeed with enough time and effort. But the owner underestimates the time needed to become profitable, and doesn't secure enough financing to survive the initial period. In this case, overconfidence dooms him.

Fearing failure is healthy to the extent it spurs me to think carefully when embracing a dream, to identify the problems I may face and prepare well for them. If you're a worrywart by nature, that can be a good thing at life's turning points, that is, if you channel your ruminations in the right direction.

Conquering Unhealthy Fears of Failure

The tragedy comes when the fear of failure frightens us away from a venture that will succeed for us. And it's here that the fear of failing far too often blinds us to life's best opportunities, and highly effectively. One reason it so easily shuts us down is because of a phenomenon known as "loss aversion." Taking a loss of any significance is demoralizing to us, and so distasteful that it affects our

well-being more greatly than succeeding. The pain we suffer at losing $1,000 is greater than the joy we experience at winning $1,000,
for instance. In the same way, the devastation of a romantic loss is
greater to us than the pleasure of a romantic success. Too often,
too, we reason outward when loss occurs, and assume the bottom is
falling out of our life at other unrelated points.

Loss aversion affects us not only as we react to past and present
disappointments, but as we envision our possibilities for success
and failure in the future. It can lead us to overestimate the possibility of failure and how it might dismantle our life. If our chances for
succeeding or failing in a given venture are equally weighed, we
attach more weight to the possibility we'll fail, and focus more on
the negative impact of a failure than on the wonderful benefits a
success could bring. The fear of failing overrides the hope of succeeding, and convinces us not to take the risk.

The fear of failure easily takes on phobic dimension as well, to
the point that even a small chance of not succeeding paralyzes us.
We fear that failure, if it did occur, would destroy us, and so even
the remote possibility must be avoided. This obsessing *is* healthy
when it comes to dangerous behavior. A one-percent chance of having an accident should be sufficient to discourage me from texting
while driving, for instance. But a one-percent likelihood a new venture will fail isn't remotely a basis not to go ahead. Failure in this
case (when the venture is highly reasonable for us and the risk of
failing low) typically isn't the monster we dread it to be, but brings
certain benefits of its own. We are far more capable of handling it
than we imagine, and over the long haul are often grateful for how
it impacts our life.

The most important step toward conquering the fear of failure,
in fact, is, well, not to fear failure. The bite of a fear is remarkably
lessened once we're persuaded that even if the worst occurred, it
wouldn't be so bad after all. Failure actually can bring us significant benefits. Appreciating failure's positive side not only reduces
our fear of it, but can give us the heart to try again if at first we

don't succeed.

While we shouldn't court failure or overtly desire it, neither should we fear it obsessively. We can find the courage to risk once we realize that even if failure occurs, we'll still benefit and be better off than if we had simply sat still.

The Benefits of Failure

Let's look at this point more closely. Failure not only helps us grow in important ways but can contribute to our eventual success, when we know how to accept a defeat and reap its benefits. There are at least three ways in which failure can benefit us.

1. Through failing we learn how to succeed. The most obvious benefit of failure is that through it our understanding grows. Through a difficult experience we learn hands-on how *not* to succeed. Lessons gleaned from experience stick with us and benefit us much more greatly than those merely learned academically. If we apply what we've learned to new challenges, our possibility of success is increased significantly. Our mistakes provide the best possible means for learning firsthand how not to do something, and thus how to better succeed in the future.

I had a hard experience in eighth grade from which I still draw benefits. A four-piece rock 'n' roll band I had formed, "The Galaxies," was scheduled to perform for an in-school talent assembly. We fully expected to give a stellar performance and be counted as class heroes for the rest of the year.

We walked on stage to tremendous applause, our heads swelling with pride. But shortly after we started our first number, my guitar amplifier went silent. The wires of my guitar cord had pulled loose from the jack plugged into the amp. An electric guitar without amplification is about as useful as a TV not turned on, and since I was the band's only melody instrument, we had no choice but to stop playing. I bent down and for several anxious minutes struggled to reattach the wires, but in my franticness snapped them off the cord. As I fumbled with that connection, the students became noisy and unruly. Finally, the principal stepped up to the microphone. He proceeded to chastise the students for being rowdy, and ordered them back to class.

Far from being heroes, our classmates looked on us as stooges who had kept them from having a good time. The shame and humiliation we felt was immense.

In time, however, I came to count this experience as one of the most beneficial of my life. Through it I discovered unforgettably the need for preparation. When a cord would break again at a future performance, I had an extra one handy to replace it. The experience touched my life in many other ways, and gave me the incentive to go the extra mile in getting ready for what I do. No text book could have taught me the lesson remotely as well.

Regardless of our age or position in life, every mistake we make has the potential to teach us critical lessons. Most of us, if we'll look honestly at our lives, will admit that certain hard experiences have done much to teach us and equip us for the quality of life we now live. Failures in relationships have taught us how to relate to people better. Failures in academic and work situations have taught us how to handle certain tasks more effectively. Failures in parenting have taught us how to better guide and encourage our children. Financial failures have given us a wiser approach to investing. Moral and spiritual defeat has taught us how to draw more fully on the power of Christ. Through all of these experiences we've come to understand our own gifts, strengths and weaknesses better, and that in turn has given us a more confident grasp of God's direction in our life.

These experiences can benefit us *if* we can take them in the right spirit. Some discouragement is normal when failure and disappointment come, and we need to allow ourselves the freedom to grieve significant losses and setbacks. Yet the point comes when we need to begin to take a more positive look at our failure and see what beneficial lessons it offers. The danger is that our failure paralyzes us. We assume failure once means failure forever.

We conclude God is against us and has shown us our fate through this unhappy experience. We lose the courage to try again.

At such times we must put into practice everything we know about the creative power of God. He is telling us to learn what we can from our failure and move on. And so often when we do, we find that vital growth has come through the experience not available any other way. A friend put it simply, that one of our chief concerns should be to learn to be a "successful failure."

Again, this principle will serve us well not only in the face of actual failure, but as we anticipate the risks involved in taking a step of faith. Even if we fail, we'll grow in certain ways that can enhance our future success. Appreciating this critical benefit makes the possibility of failure less threatening.

2. Failure can carry a success of its own. A second point to remember is that experiences we deem failures sometimes turn out to be successes in the long run. We find we called the shots wrong.

Christian psychiatrist Paul Tournier writes about one of his most humiliating experiences, which occurred when he was speaking at a university:

I felt right from the first word that I was not going to make contact with my audience. I clung to my notes and laboriously recited, with growing nervousness, what I had to say. As the audience left I could see my friends slipping hurriedly away. . . . On the way home in my car with my wife, I burst into tears.[2]

The next day, a philosophy professor phoned him, saying that the talk was indeed the worst he had ever heard. But he added that while he had sat through numerous erudite lectures in his lifetime that had left no impression, he was somehow drawn to Tournier. A lasting friendship developed between the two, which resulted in the professor's coming to Christ. Tournier now looks back upon that embarrassing lecture as one of the great successes of his life.

Tournier's experience reminds us that failure can have more than just educational value. It may also be a success we don't yet recognize. There are times we fail to live up to our own expectations and yet fulfill God's quite well. What we perceive as a failure may be a success in his mind, contributing positively to our future and to his intentions for our life. God understands success much better than we do.

Tournier's story also brings out how God honors our honest efforts at success, often in ways we don't at first recognize. And it reminds us that the experience we perceive as a failure may provide a pathway to a personal victory. The process that brings disappointment also brings certain positive momentum, which helps to open unexpected doors. It allows us to meet certain people who end up helping us. And it puts us in new situations that in time position us to succeed.

After graduating from college with a teaching degree, a friend of mine, Janet, accepted a job at a Maryland middle school. She soon felt like a fish out of water there. Having grown up in a rural area many hours away, Janet found the culture of the region where she now taught—a Washington, D.C. suburb—too chaotic. She resolved to leave by the school year's end, if not before, and ranked this job choice as a failure. Until . . . she met the band teacher, to whom she is now happily married. Janet now rates her decision to work at this school as, well, a great success.

This is perhaps the most common way a failure morphs into a success for us. We fail to reach a certain cherished goal. But we've kept our life in motion, and through that movement has come an unexpected and perhaps life-changing benefit.

This staying-in-motion factor can work for us in a different way, by allowing us to cooperate with God's timing. While we fail to realize our initial goal, the process of trying occupies us for a while. When we then try something new, we enjoy a blessing that wouldn't have come if we had taken our new direction earlier. The time taken up pursuing our failed goal positioned us for good timing when we took this new step of faith.

And so it was that Malcolm, the band teacher whom Janet met and married, spent the previous year, his first one teaching, in an unsatisfying job. He had longed to teach middle or high school band, but the county gave him an elementary school position teaching general music. It was a difficult job for Malcolm, who wanted to teach older students, and it required shuffling between two schools. But the year taken up with that unhappy assignment positioned Malcolm for stunning timing when a middle school position finally opened the next year, for it was the year—and likely the only one— that Janet was teaching there.

Examples like Tournier's, Janet's, and Malcolm's give us pause to be careful not to label a disappointment a failure until we've seen the long-term results. Appreciating how a failure can become a success can help to quell our fear of failing enough to take some reasonable risks.

3. It sometimes takes a certain number of failures to bring about a success. This third benefit of failure is more mystical and difficult to pin down. Yet it's no less important to understand. There seems to be a law in human life that success often comes only through a number of earnest attempts. It sometimes takes a number of failures to breed a success. It's the principle of sowing seeds that is talked about so frequently in Scripture. Some seeds take root while others do not, for reasons we never fully understand. Yet the greater the number sown, the stronger the likelihood of a rich harvest. Thus, Scripture declares,

> As you do not know the path of the wind, or how the body is formed in a mother's womb, so you cannot understand the work of God, the Maker of all things. Sow your seed in the morning, and at evening let not your hands be idle, for you do not know which will succeed, whether this or that, or whether both will do equally well. (Eccles 11:5-6)

Sometimes failure does mean we've made mistakes. As we examine our experience we discover what we did wrong and how to avoid the same errors in the future. We learn from our failure and grow through it. Yet in other cases we're not able to discern clear mistakes. Our failure seems to have come about in spite of doing everything right. At such times we're especially prone to self-disparagement, for the evidence seems to suggest God has cast the lots against us. We become fatalistic and conclude that God doesn't want us to succeed in this particular area. We lose the courage to try again.

The fact is we don't know the mind of God. Usually we have very little basis for judging whether he is punishing us through a failure or not. The possibility is just as real that the failure suggests only that God's time for success hasn't yet come for us. By the principle of sowing seeds, success isn't less likely now, but *more* so! If we'll simply keep casting the seeds, eventually one will take root. It's fair to think of this, too, as a principle of compensation. Failure with one try is compensated for by success with another.

Genesis records a time when Isaac and his servants made three attempts to dig for water in the valley of Gerar (Gen 26:19-22). After each of the first two, native herdsmen quarreled with them over property rights, and Isaac's men had to abandon the wells after all the strenuous effort digging them. But the third time they succeeded and encountered no resistance. Isaac named the well Rehoboth ("a broad place"), declaring, "Now the LORD has given us room and we will flourish in the land." Less hardy souls would have given up after the first or second attempt, saying, "God doesn't intend that I succeed."

The principle of sowing seeds seems to be an aspect of God's common grace and his dealing with all people, and one that touches everyone in important ways. In their classic *In Search of Excellence,* Thomas Peters and Robert Waterman note that repeated effort is one of the most common keys to success among notable businesses. The oil companies most successful in discovering oil, for instance, aren't the ones with the best equipment or the most intelligent personnel, but the ones who dig the most wells! Persistence is the factor separating the successful firms from the unsuccessful ones.[3]

Yet the principle is also one that applies to the Christian's walk of faith. Even a man as spiritually mature as the apostle Paul some-times had to make several bungled attempts before finally enjoy-ing an opening to use his gifts for Christ (as we noted earlier in Acts 16:6-10).

I've experienced the sowing-seeds principle often in musical performing. With the band I'm currently in, for instance, we have good nights and bad ones—a good night being where a restaurant we're playing in is filled with enthusiastic people, and a bad night when we're, well, playing to the walls. And it can vary a lot. At a restaurant where we currently perform, the crowd is sometimes somewhat thin. But on a recent Saturday night, a line of people waited to be seated, and the packed audience cheered us on like heroes. And yet there often seems no rhyme or reason to these dif-ferences between gigs. Since many random factors affect attendance on any given evening, there's always hope the next performance will be better attended than the last.

Of the principles of success and failure we're considering, this is perhaps the most important to keep in mind in romantic relation-ships. I've counseled many singles who've suffered several disap-pointments and are now ready to throw in the towel. They're convinced their chances of marrying are null and that past failures prove God hasn't cut them out for marriage. Seldom do I believe this conclusion is justified. In the immensely complex world of ro-mantic relationships, the chemistry that's absent in one case thrives wonderfully and surprisingly in another.

God's timetable with each of us is remarkably different, and we shouldn't assume that disappointment in the past means we're doomed to it forever. There may be lessons to learn from past dis-appointments. But in many cases the failure of romance to flourish simply means that compatibility wasn't right, and you couldn't have done anything to change that. In another relationship the mix of factors will be different and compatibility much more natural.

When disappointment in romance comes, we should, to be sure, pray that God will give us the heart to accept it and move on. But

praying for acceptance of the present isn't incompatible with praying for change in the future. If your desire for marriage continues to
be strong, you should express it to God honestly and continue to be
hopeful that the opportunity will come.

In romance, and in other areas too, we need to be careful not to
become fatalistic about the future because of past failure. Particularly when no clear lessons can be learned from a disappointment,
the principle of casting seeds suggests we should stay hopeful. Failure in the past may just as well indicate we're now in line for a
victory as anything! The important thing is not to lose heart. We
must not close the door in any area of our life before God is ready
to do so.

Not Giving up on Important Dreams
Last week I gave a homily at the wedding of a dear friend of over
30 years. She has earnestly desired to be married for most of this
time, and in recent years relentlessly pursued options through
eHarmony. The result? She was "closed" over 150 times, suffered
through a number of unsatisfying face-to-face meetings, and endured some short-lived relationships. Yet about two years ago her
persistence with online matching finally paid off, and she met the
man whom she just married, a superb match for her. Her success is
thrilling to me, and deeply reassuring about the value of persistence in finding someone to marry.

Hers is a role model for you to consider. While she didn't enjoy
her many disappointments, any more than any of us would, she
conquered her fear of failure enough to keep trying till she succeeded. By learning to stare fear down, and by staying tenacious,
she achieved her dream.

For each of us, the critical question with any venture we consider is, do I have a reasonable chance of succeeding? If so, then
we should go ahead, trusting that if we don't succeed, our failure
will bring certain benefits that still make the effort worthwhile. When
I say "a reasonable chance of success," I'm referring to the broad

dream we're pursuing, such as the desire to find someone to marry. In such a quest, we'll probably need to take many intermediate steps that are more risky, like my friend's numerous efforts through eHarmony, en route to achieving a dream that itself is wholly reasonable.

One goal that is totally reasonable is mastering the fear of failure itself. It *can* be done. We *can* learn to be resilient in the face of failure, and even comfortable with it, especially when the dream we're pursuing is reasonable to begin with. Learning to focus on the potential benefits of failure is a giant step toward conquering our fear.

8

The Fear of Success

Agreat aunt of mine, after finishing high school, enrolled in college. She faithfully pursued her academic program for nearly four years. Then, two weeks before graduation—she quit. Although only a few assignments remained, she claimed she had lost interest and saw no purpose in completing the degree.

My aunt's stunning decision demonstrates one of human nature's greatest ironies. Even when a goal is achievable for us, we may still bail out, or do something so counterproductive that it prevents our success. Our uneasiness with succeeding can lead us to sabotage dreams that are well within our reach.

As dearly as we may long for success on one level, we may dread it on another. If our wariness doesn't spur us to do something insidious to thwart our achievement, it may still prevent us from truly enjoying it or from fully reaping its benefits.

My aunt's behavior was extreme, unquestionably. The actions we may take to derail a dream, or to dampen our joy in succeeding, are often more subtle and ingenious. They're often so subconsciously driven that we fail to recognize we've sabotaged our goal. Have you ever caught a cold just before giving a talk or vocal performance? Suffered an accident en route to a job interview or important meeting? Had a falling out over something minor with someone in a position to help you? Such incidents can indicate you're uneasy with success.

I say *can,* for the fact we suffer a setback doesn't necessarily mean we fear succeeding or are being restrained subconsciously. Yet our fear of success can induce our subconscious to act against us.

Like the fear of failure, the fear of success can keep us from taking important steps of faith and squelch our efforts to make needed changes. And for many, it's even more effective than the fear of failure at shutting them down. Yet the fear of success is far less understood and appreciated than the fear of failure, and many motivational books do not discuss it at all. If we're going to realize our full potential for Christ, it's vital to understand our potential to fear success, and to be ready to tame our anxieties about succeeding. And so I want to look at the problem carefully now. (I discuss the fear of success in *The Yes Anxiety* and *Reach Beyond Your Grasp,* and draw on material from these books in this chapter.[1])

Peter's Example

We find an enlightening example of the fear of success in one of the early encounters that Peter and his friends had with Jesus, described in Luke 5:1-11. They had fished all night yet caught nothing. Jesus tells them to drop their nets once again, and this time their catch is so huge that they can scarcely haul it ashore. Peter then declares to Jesus, "Go away from me, Lord; I am a sinful man!" (v 8).

We would have expected Peter and his friends to be elated over their unexpected triumph. Such an overwhelming catch of fish is a fisherman's dream. They surely would want Jesus to give them this success again and again.

Instead, they were taken drastically off guard by this sudden, inexplicable feat. They had grown accustomed to failure, and success was a jolt to their comfort zone. They felt morbidly unworthy of it. They undoubtedly feared that as Jesus came to know them better, he would judge them fraudulent and use this same miraculous power to destroy them.

Jesus, in magnanimous compassion and grace, ignored Peter's self-defeating request (thank God he often ignores our misguided prayers). He assured Peter and his friends that he intended *more* success for them, and on a more meaningful level. "Don't be afraid; from now on you will fish for people" (v 10). His response clearly calmed the disciples' fears. They were so relieved to find he had positive intentions for them that "they pulled their boats up on shore, left everything and followed him" (v 11).

I'm certain that high among Jesus' greatest healing miracles was giving his early followers victory over their fears of success. He inspired within them the spiritual and psychological strength to bound beyond the inertia of their routine existence into the dynamic life of following him. In Peter the change was nothing short of revolutionary. On the day of Pentecost this man who had been plagued with inferiority stood up and forcefully addressed the multitude, convincing many to repent and follow Christ. Later, even the Jewish authorities were astonished "when they saw the courage of Peter and John and realized that they were unschooled, ordinary men" (Acts 4:13).

If you're fearful of success, take heart. You're not alone. This is an area of struggle for many. Christ understands your predicament. As surely as he has saved you, he can give you the grace to overcome this fear and realize your full potential for him.

Why We Fear Success
Let's look more closely at what characterizes the fear of success. There are certain common anxieties that many experience in anticipation of reaching a goal.

1. The fear of losing others' approval. I don't know what prompted my aunt, long deceased, to opt out of college so close to finishing. I do have a strong suspicion. It was unusual enough for a woman to attend college in the early 1900s, let alone graduate. She may have feared others would think her too driven by masculine instincts if she gained the degree. Marriage suitors might be frightened away.

If I'm right, then she demonstrates one of the most common reasons we dread success: we fear offending others whose affection we prize.

While the social climate has improved radically for woman in the century since my aunt abandoned college, many still worry that success will hinder their romantic aspirations. Will that promotion or advanced degree work against me in relationships? Will it alienate the man who wants to feel superior, or who's looking for a woman more drawn to domestic life?

Both men and women worry about the impact of success on friendships and family relationships. Will those who love me as I am now still like me as much if I succeed? Will they think I've acted pridefully by pursuing my dream? Will they be offended or withdraw their affection—even in subtle ways?

If such concerns grow strong enough, we may let a dream go, even though our prospects for success are good.

2. The fear of one-upping others. We may also feel uneasy about succeeding in an area where a family member or close friend has failed. Our success might cause them to feel the pain of their failure even more greatly, we imagine, and so we fear hurting them. Even if this person is rooting for us to succeed, we may still feel it's inappropriate to allow ourselves to enjoy a benefit they failed to attain.

In her mammoth fifteen-year study of the effects of divorce on children, Judith Wallerstein observes that women whose mothers suffered a failed marriage often feel guilty availing themselves of a good opportunity to marry. It isn't fair to let themselves enjoy bliss that mom didn't.[2]

Men may also hold back from marriage out of a similar concern of hurting their father. More typically, though, they fear one-upping him professionally, and may feel guilty excelling in a career where he failed.

3. Breaking the comfort zone of failure. A more subtle problem occurs if we experienced failure while growing up, to the point we became accustomed to not succeeding. Failure may now be such a familiar experience that we feel uncomfortable breaking its inertia.

The challenge can be especially great if we were *rewarded* for failing. A child may find his problems bring him more welcome attention than his achievements. Take Sarah, a fifth grader, whose parents have an unstable marriage. Her folks are so preoccupied with their own problems that, when she brings home good marks, they scarcely notice. Yet when the principal phones to tell them Sarah skipped school, they stop fighting long enough to focus on helping her work through her problems. Sarah not only cherishes the attention, but relishes the fact that her misbehavior has encouraged at least temporary harmony between her parents.

If a child has enough experiences like this, she may grow to regard failure as rewarding. "If I succeed, who notices?" she thinks; "if I fail, I'm consoled." As an adult, she may strongly want to succeed in certain areas, yet be held back by the force of these expectations established in childhood, which are now largely subconscious.

4. The fear of punishment from God. The most crippling anxiety some people suffer about success is that God will punish them if they reach their goal. God knows they don't deserve to succeed, they assume. He won't like it if they do. He will crown their victory with misfortune.

The fear of God's punishment for succeeding is a natural human instinct, and more deeply imbedded than many realize. So much so, that many primitive religions have rituals for appeasing the gods upon achieving personal success.

In *Overcoming the Fear of Success*, therapist Martha Freedman tells of a carpenter she counseled who, fulfilling a life's dream, worked diligently at building a first-class racing boat. Yet he couldn't bring himself to apply the final coat of paint, fearing once he completed his project, he would die. The story does have a happy ending. With Freedman's help, he found the courage to take that step. He didn't die or suffer disaster. To the contrary, he found succeeding so exhilarating that it inspired him to launch a career building master racing craft. Yet his example shows how insidiously the fear of God's punishment can blunt our creative output.[3]

It's not unusual for Christians, who believe strongly in the grace and forgiveness of God, and in his rewards for obedience, to also fear his displeasure over achieving personal dreams. We're inconsistent creatures, and may even believe that God is calling us to pursue a goal and, yet at the same time fear his chastisement if we succeed.

5. An excessive concern with owning our own life. Another reason we may resist success illustrates one of the most debilitating ways our psyche can function. We may feel uneasy achieving a goal because we know others *want* us to reach it. Our need for control is so great that we want to avoid any semblance of living out others' expectations—even *positive* ones. We don't want to give anyone the gratification of rejoicing in our success, or of thinking they helped us by cheering us on.

It's not unusual, for instance, for a grown son or daughter to choose a career different from the one their parents wish, even if he or she would otherwise prefer that option.

When our concern with owning our life is healthy, we naturally wish to act against others' negative expectations. When we feel compelled to defy their *positive* expectations, we've taken the need to own our life to an unfortunate level. At this point, we may feel uneasy succeeding in any way at all, for it's difficult to find any worthy goal that at least someone isn't rooting for us to achieve.

6. The fear of increased responsibility and losing freedom.

There's also a reason we can fear success that isn't complicated or difficult to understand at all. We worry that the increased responsibilities of reaching a goal will be too burdensome. While this fear is sometimes justified, it often amounts to focusing too greatly on the challenges of achieving a dream, rather than on the benefits.

Success typically reduces our freedom in certain ways, and that concern can also be unsettling. We don't like having our options reduced in any way, and we exhilarate in being as broadly free to choose as possible. The fear of losing freedom is the most common reason people who dearly want to be married still opt out of good opportunities. It's also why many fail to pursue golden prospects in career and other areas.

7. *The fear of insignificance.* At the same time, we can be hampered by a rather different concern—that what we accomplish may be of no ultimate significance to human life anyway. Why bother to make the effort? So what if I slave to put myself through college and pull top grades as an economics major? So what if I land a good position with a corporation? What will I achieve that someone else couldn't accomplish just as well?

What difference will it make if we have a second child? Billions of children have come into existence and died throughout history without making any impact on the world.

We are complex psychological creatures and often experience conflicting fears at the same time. One moment the thought of completing a goal unsettles us because we fear it will elevate us to more importance than we deserve. The next moment we're sapped by the thought that, even if we succeed, our achievement won't dent the world's problems.

Turning the Tide

While there are other reasons we may fear success, these are some of the major ones. They're enough to show that we humans are complex psychologically, and may desire success greatly on one level, yet resist it on another. Even if we're not vulnerable in most of these ways, we may still be at one or more, to the point that we sabotage good opportunities or fail to benefit fully from our victories.

The good news is we can fight back. We can change self-defeating patterns, and even reverse tendencies that thwart our dreams.

If you're uncomfortable with success, can you clarify why? Consider the seven reasons I've suggested, and see if any of these shoes fit. Can you identify certain outlooks that diminish your zeal to succeed? Write them down. Be as specific as you can.

Perhaps you avoid success for reasons you *can't* clearly specify. You only know that you fall into the same self-defeating behavior time and again, but don't understand why. If so, then I urge you to seek a professional's help. You're dealing with a formidable problem that you're unlikely to conquer on your own. With a counselor's direction, you can identify factors that have programmed you instinctively to court failure rather than success. Most important, you can determine steps that will change the pattern, and allow you to begin following your dreams more effectively.

Paradigm Shifts Regarding Success

You may be only too aware of why you dread success. Certain conscious assumptions discourage you, and you quickly identify with one or more of the unhealthy patterns of thinking I've just discussed. You may not need professional counseling to untangle deep-seated complexes. You do need to develop more healthy thinking about success, and to revise perspectives that are working against you. Here are some outlooks that can help.

• *Too much significance—or too little?* Since the anticipation of success can fill us with fears of both significance and insignificance, we need to learn to hold on to two perspectives at once. On the one hand, we should remind ourselves that Christ has a distinctive plan for our life. He has given us a combination of gifts and opportunities as unique from anyone else's as our fingerprints. The work we do may seem futile in a purely objective sense. Yes, we may take a job that could easily be filled by someone else. Still, our personality and mix of gifts will allow us to relate to certain people for Christ within our work in ways no one else is as well-equipped to do. And, in the mystery of God's providence, we'll be there at just the right moment to meet certain needs of people that otherwise would go unheeded.

But a sense of futility can keep us from taking the steps so critical to keeping pace with his will. We must remind ourselves constantly that God's plan for us is personally designed so that the work we accomplish will contribute significantly to what Christ is doing to meet other's needs. God intends our life as a matchless gift to people. Others will be deprived of important benefits if we fail to act.

At the same time, we should remind ourselves that ultimately our work is only one small part of the picture of all that God is doing. We'll make plenty of mistakes, and the world won't expire as a result! Ultimately the work is God's, anyway, and we're forever in danger of taking ourselves too seriously.

In *Overcoming the Fear of Success,* psychologist Martha Friedman shares her own struggle with success as a doctoral candidate and how she conquered it:

> I was on the verge of becoming a Ph.D. dropout when a wise psychologist said to me, "Why such a fuss? Nobody's going to read it anyway; it'll just gather dust on some college library shelf, and it'll certainly never be published. If you're meant to do important work, you'll do it after you get out of school."
>
> I stopped obsessing, took a month off from my jobs, and finished my dissertation. While it's admittedly no major contribution to world science, it was a major contribution to my psyche. I had finished something important to me. It was . . . a matter of not magnifying what I was trying to accomplish.

She adds, "Minimizing the importance of a goal is an excellent way to reach that goal."[4]

We each need to work at achieving a healthy balance in the way we perceive our work. We need to know that what we do is significant; yet we must remember that we're instruments of a God who uses our weaknesses as effectively as our strengths. In Christ, we can achieve this balance, for we can know that while our work is an important part of the help he extends to the world, he doesn't ultimately *depend* upon us but graciously uses our availability. With this knowledge, we can serve in a spirit of joyous victory, not defeat.

• *God's will and my success.* The belief that God may punish us for succeeding usually springs from humility that, in itself, is commendable. As Christians, we're only too aware that our motives, even in pursuing the noblest goal, are mixed at best. As we grow in Christ, we become more conscious of unhealthy motives—a function of coming closer to his light and being exposed by it. And recognizing that our motives are less than perfect may lead us to fear God's retribution if we succeed.

Scripture also stresses that we shouldn't cherish grandiose ideas about ourselves (Rom 12:3, Phil 2:3), and warns us constantly to be on guard against any attraction becoming an idol.

Yet failure, in its own strange way, can become an idol to us—every bit as greatly as success. And our motives in courting failure can be just as unhealthy as in chasing some totally selfish goal.

In pursuing any dream, we should strive to keep our relationship with Christ strong, and pray earnestly that God will give us motives honoring to Christ. Yet, as Paul reminds us graphically in Romans 7, we can never rid ourselves fully of selfish intentions this side of eternity. If we let ourselves be obsessed with motives, we'll become convinced we're unworthy of any accomplishment, and be immobilized.

Our life is of far greater benefit to others—and to Christ's mission—when we focus our energy primarily, not upon motives, but upon realizing our best potential for Christ. Consider that Paul, in his extensive teaching on spiritual gifts, never tells believers to refrain from using their gifts because of imperfect motives. He consistently counsels us to diligently employ our gifts for the benefit of others. He surely recognized that our motives would sometimes be less than ideal in this process.

Scripture not only teaches that God gives us potential and golden opportunities, but that he wants us to *rejoice* in our successes. The Israelites were instructed to set aside a tithe of their produce to eat before the Lord in a spirit of celebration (Deut 12:5-19, 14:22-27). They were *commanded* to rejoice over what God had enabled them to accomplish! The stunning implication is that God takes joy in our accomplishments and wishes to rejoice with us in our victories.

God desires not that we deny our personal dreams, but that we pursue them *in companionship with him*. He wants us to pursue a dream as an odyssey traveled with him—an adventure where we seek his guidance, strength and provision, and then rejoice with him in our successes. When we imagine God being against our succeeding, we're thinking of him as our adversary rather than our friend. Nothing helps more to combat our fears of success than to appreciate God as our companion who is cheering us on as we move toward our goals.

• *Will others disapprove or be hurt by my succeeding?* In developing a healthy outlook on success, we also need to come to terms with concerns about others' reactions. The perception that others don't want us to succeed sometimes has basis. But remember that God has made human nature remarkably resilient. We can bear the disappointment of lost affection if something positive takes its place. It can be a worthwhile tradeoff to let go of some affirmation in order to experience the joy of using our gifts more fully. And as we take steps of growth, we best position ourselves to develop new friendships. In the long run, we're happier in relationships with those who desire God's best for us than with those who insist we conform to their still-life pictures.

But what about the fear that our success will dishearten our parents or others who are discouraged about their own failures?

The concern not to hurt others by outshining them can spring from compassion, respect, and a genuine desire to promote their welfare. Still, it's always a case of assuming responsibility that isn't properly ours, and indicates we've been drawn in to a codependent mentality. Following Christ means learning not only to trust our own life into his hands, but others' lives as well.

If my success causes my parents or anyone else to feel dejected, they're basing their self-worth on the wrong factors to begin with. They need to grow, rather than for me to adjust my plans to their expectations. They'll only be fulfilled when they accept God's unique plan for them and learn to make the best of their own opportunities. Until they stop measuring their happiness against others' successes and failures, they're doomed to stay frustrated. I'm not helping them change by accommodating their unhealthy outlook, but am helping it become more deeply ingrained. I'll best serve them by refusing to let their attitude dampen my zeal. I should remember, too, that, beyond these people, many others will benefit from my success, for it will better equip me to serve their needs. I will best love them by pursuing my dream.

• *Living out others' positive expectations.* But what if my determination to own my life is so great that I'm ruffled even by the thought of fulfilling others' positive expectations? I need to begin by recognizing the sheer futility of my position. Since it's unlikely I'll accomplish any worthwhile goal without pleasing at least some people, I'm effectively blocking myself from achieving any personal dream.

I also need to redefine what it means to own my own life. Rather than think, "I'll avoid living out others' expectations at any cost," I should determine, "I'm going to realize my dreams regardless of what anyone thinks. If someone is gratified by my victory, or believes their well-wishes have helped me succeed, let them think whatever they want. I won't let anyone's expectations—positive or negative—deter me from doing what's right for me."

I should pray also that God will help me keep the urge to own my life within reasonable bounds. A moderate desire to own our life serves us much better than an extreme one.

• *Bearing the burden.* We may also worry that success will saddle us with responsibility too burdensome for us. This fear is sometimes justified, and helps guard us against a "rescue" mentality. Yet it is often unreasonable, and may hold us back from opportunities that will truly improve our life.

How, then, can we determine if our apprehensions are reasonable? We should look honestly at what our real concern is. Am I worried that success will bring with it *too much* responsibility? Or am I more concerned about being able to handle the responsibility psychologically?

Will success so tax my time and energy, for instance, that it jeopardizes my family life or other important commitments? If so, then I need to address the problem carefully. Is it possible to delegate responsibility, so that I'm able to accomplish more with the same effort? Often the answer is yes. But if the answer is clearly no, then I shouldn't pursue my dream until I'm certain I can handle its duties without unhealthy tradeoffs.

Often, though, our real concern is whether we can psychologically handle new responsibility that otherwise fits the limits of our time and energy fine. A job I'm offered requires public speaking, for instance, which frightens me. In this case, I should see the new opportunity as a chance to grow. I should recall past occasions when God gave me strength under fire that I thought wasn't possible for me. I should remind myself constantly that this same God will support me in my new challenges. I have a remarkable opportunity to reach new horizons—both in faith and in personal skill.

If an opportunity otherwise matches me well, and doesn't tax my time and energy unreasonably, I should see its psychological challenges as occasions to rise to, and open myself to God's new adventure. In this case, I benefit far more greatly by staring fear down than by caving in.

• *A tradeoff worth making.* What often worries us most about new responsibility isn't that it will be too burdensome or psychologically challenging, but that we'll lose freedom by taking it on. Regardless how strongly we desire the benefits an opportunity offers, committing to it means forsaking other choices. Some people dwell so much on the freedom they'll lose by achieving even a cherished dream that they conclude the tradeoff isn't worth it.

It helps to remember the problem of loss aversion, which we looked at in the last chapter. We humans instinctively invest greater emotion in losses than we do in gains of equal value. The sorrow we feel over losing a sum of money is greater than our pleasure over winning the same amount. Our devastation in losing a friendship is stronger than our joy in gaining a new friendship. And we can focus so greatly on what we have to give up to reach a goal, that success feels more like failure.

The best way to fight this tendency is to make a determined effort to concentrate on the benefits of accomplishing our dream. The man, for instance, who feels weak-kneed about committing to marriage, even in the face of a welcome opportunity, should focus as fully as he can upon the improvements it will bring to his life. He may find it helpful to take a personal retreat, where he dwells on these advantages, and gives God an unhindered opportunity to deepen his passion for being married.

Meditating on the benefits of taking any step of faith will help us break the pull of loss aversion, and find the courage to move toward our dream.

* * * * * * * *

Do you have a history of bailing out of welcome opportunities? Do you often avoid victories that are within your reach? If you instinctively tend to thwart your own good fortune, look closely at whether a fear of success, rather than failure, is the cause. If so, then focus more on this chapter than any other in this book. Carefully consider the ways you can fear success that I've outlined, and try to identify precisely what it is about succeeding that you personally dread.

Then strive to revise your thinking about success, however you need to, along the lines I've suggested. And commit to a dream and follow it through, no matter how much fear and trembling you have to endure. Make it your goal to sabotage your tendency to sabotage your dreams. The great news is that this goal is achievable! Take heart, especially, in knowing that God is on your side as you seek to reinvent your attitude toward success, and to realize your greatest potential for Christ.

9

The Fear of
Commitment

The fear of failure. The fear of success. It might seem these are the sum and total of all the apprehensions we can suffer when considering a major step with our life.

But wait, there's more.

We can also fear commitment. Most simply described, commitment fear is feeling claustrophobic about the step we're considering. It's the dread of being locked in to this new situation, with no easy escape, and losing our freedom to chose other options. We feel trapped at the thought of being obligated, like being stuck in an elevator. We feel profoundly uncomfortable about being, well, committed.

Commitment anxiety can dog us in any decision. We may disdain the thought of being locked in to a college major, a career, a certain job, membership in a church or community organization, a self-improvement goal, a purchase decision or the promise to spend time with someone. Yet in these cases commitment fear usually isn't so intense that it unravels us. And we can often get beyond it simply by "growing up" a bit—that is, by facing life's finite nature and our need to be decisive.

Enter, though, the decision to get married. Here the fear of commitment can strike with a vengeance, and so intensely that a woman breaks an engagement she had agreed to joyfully, cancels wedding plans and backs away from a cherished opportunity to marry. In a more positive case, a man may stay the course to marriage, but with the excitement of a patient facing major surgery. Commitment fear can be truly disabling when facing marriage, and is a deal-killer for many. I'm going to focus mainly on the marriage decision in this chapter, for this is where a golden opportunity is most often squashed by commitment anxiety.

It took me some time to wake up to what a serious problem commitment anxiety is for many considering marriage. In 1988 I contracted with InterVarsity Press to write a book on the marriage decision. The concern was to help Christians—especially those already in serious relationships—decide whether to marry. I produced a manuscript covering every angle of the matter I could think of, and submitted it. The editors liked what I had so far, but had one further suggestion. Would I add a section on the fear of commitment? With all the attention I had given my topic, it had never dawned on me to address this issue. But to keep them happy, I agreed. For perspective, I read one book, *Men Who Can't Love: How to Recognize a Commitmentphobic Man Before He Breaks Your Heart*, by Steven Carter and Julia Sokol. Then over a weekend I whittled out a section on commitment fear, that was tacked on to the end of my book, almost like an appendix.

Once *Should I Get Married?* was published, I was surprised to find that this hastily-added section generated the greatest interest. Most readers who contacted me wanted help in overcoming commitment anxiety. This wake-up call spurred me to write a book exclusively on the subject—*The Yes Anxiety: Taming the Fear of Commitment*, published in 1994—and then to publish a revised edition of *Should I Get Married?* in 2000 with an expanded section on the fear of commitment. With the advent of the Internet, and to this day, most who email me after reading any of my books are seeking counsel about commitment fear.

An Intense Fear for Many

Those concerned enough to email me or speak with me about their commitment fear usually describe it in the most dramatic terms. They speak of frequent anxiety attacks, rapid heartbeat, difficulty eating, stomach pain, dizziness and sleeplessness. A friend recently told me he had been so frightened of marrying that he didn't sleep during the two weeks prior to his wedding. I should hasten to note that he has been happily married now for ten years, and his experience—like that of countless others I've known—points out how highly deceptive commitment fear typically is. Hearing this is cold comfort to the one in its grip, though, who assumes their fear is a life sentence. Breaking their engagement seems the only path to relief.

The commitment anxiety most describe to me is clearly at a phobic level. Carter and Sokol weren't exaggerating when they spoke of "commitmentphobia," as many truly fear commitment this greatly. A phobia, as we've noted, is a fear that has spiraled wholly out of control, and is drastically out of proportion to any true risk involved. Some of us are simply wired emotionally to be phobic about commitment. Identifying commitment fear as a phobia, when it has reached this level, is a critical step toward understanding and conquering it.

Because phobic fear is intense and painful, for instance, many naturally repress it when the situation they fear isn't present, and they don't appreciate how susceptible they are. One who fears air travel may fantasize about flying away to exotic destinations, but once they schedule a flight, panic sets in. This helps explain why many are stunned to find they dread commitment, and baffled by the fears they suffer. One may long to marry someone, and commit to marry them with joy and high expectations, but then be gripped with panic a day or two later. Some start obsessing about the other's imperfections or the possibility of a failed marriage. Many, though, cannot identify any serious problem of their partner's that is triggering their fear. They may even speak in glowing terms about this person, and how from every rational angle they've found their ideal match. They simply know they're traumatized at the thought of being *obligated* to this individual for life.

Am I Missing God's Best?

Those who are able to articulate a reason why they dread being locked in to a relationship with someone they love and cherish, typically cite one reason above all others. They worry that someone might be out there who is even better suited for them. If they waited a little longer and searched a bit further, they might find someone they haven't yet met who would be a better match and better qualified to be their life companion. How can they know they've found the right person, when they've met only a tiny fraction of the potential candidates?

Here we get to the heart of why commitment fear is so widespread today and so unique to our modern age. It's indeed true that if you searched further, you could probably find another wonderful person willing to marry you, and possibly many such candidates. And it's totally possible you might find someone better matched to you than your current partner—that's a fair assumption. The ease of mobility we enjoy today makes these possibilities all too real, and it's only natural to fear you haven't done everything you can to find your perfect mate.

This point sunk in strongly when I was writing the commitment fear portion of *Should I Get Married?*, and then *The Yes Anxiety, in 1989 and 1993*. Western society had become extraordinarily mobile by this point in the late twentieth century. Had you lived just a generation or two before, you would likely have lived out your adult years and expired in the same town or region where you were born and raised. And you probably would have *married* someone from that vicinity as well. You may have dated a few people en route to finding your spouse. But by your early or mid-twenties, you would have felt you had exhausted the pool of candidates enough to be confident of finding a suitable match. Because travel and long-distance communication were much more difficult then, you were less vulnerable to musing about someone better waiting for you in another city. And the comfort of marrying someone from your own region, who shared your history, trumped more exotic possibilities in distant ports.

By the late twentieth century, these dynamics had drastically changed. Society was so highly mobile now that you were likely to make at least several major moves in your lifetime, and far less likely to travel from the cradle to the grave in the same small town. You could drive anywhere in the U.S. within a few days, fly there within a few hours—and to any distant region in the world within a day or two. Consider the stark difference: in 1990 you could fly from Washington, D.C. to Paris in seven hours; in 1790 that same trip took one-to-two months—if you were fortunate to reach your destination at all. And no matter where you lived in America, inexpensive and reliable long-distance phone service was at your fingertips. It was now exquisitely easy to plant your feet in a distant city and explore the possibilities for romance, and even easier to pick up a phone and call someone there.

If you lived in a metropolitan area, you could also stay put and enjoy its high mobility, with people moving and traveling there constantly. And so wait a bit longer, and your ideal mate might just show up at your doorstep.

It's hard to exaggerate how this growth in mobility and telecommunication changed the way we think about finding someone to marry. Now it was hard for a thinking woman to believe that her search Mr. Right was really over. There was still this mammoth field white-unto-harvest waiting to be explored. Add to this the advent of Hollywood media and television, constantly parading before us images of the most attractive and compelling personalities who walk this earth. They so quickly and subtly became the model for our fantasies about the ideal mate, and the standard by which real-life possibilities were judged.

When you add the impact of modern media to the ease of mobility and communication we enjoy today, the wonder isn't that some people fear committing to marriage, but why everyone doesn't. There are so many reasons to make you question whether you've really found your best possible match. If you give it more time and search more carefully, might you do better? And have you really set your standards high enough? These factors impressed me strongly when I was writing those books, and helped me appreciate why commitment anxiety was so pervasive among singles I was teaching and counseling.

Internet Options Can Increase Commitment Fear

And all of this was . . . before the dawn of the Internet. By the late twentieth century, singles had substantial reasons to doubt their marriage choice, and would today even if the Internet had never emerged. But factor in its influence, and especially the proliferation of online dating and matching services, and the challenge increases exponentially. Don't get me wrong; sites such as eHarmony and match.com do a world of good for those seeking a spouse, and many find excellent matches through them. But these marvelous services are one more factor—and a major one—that leave us wondering if we've turned over every stone in looking for the right person to marry.

Until recently, my son Ben lived in Port Allegany, a small town in mountainous north-central Pennsylvania, a remote region two hours from the nearest large city. Never mind its isolation. A neighbor of Ben's who grew up in this town is now happily married to an Australian man, who lives with her in her Port Allegany home. It was through eHarmony that she met this man, half a world away, whom she connected with initially without leaving her home. Of course, we all know of stories like this—they're commonplace now.

But the fact such unlikely matches occur so often, and so effort-lessly for some, only leaves the commitment-fearful more anxious. A vast new world of possible partners is accessible now through our computer's keyboard or our smartphone's touchpad. How can I ever know if I've searched diligently enough for the right person?

Overcoming Commitment Anxiety

It's not hard to understand, then, why committing to marriage con-fidently is difficult for many today. No matter how superbly matched you seem to be with someone, it's natural to wonder if someone is out there who fits you better. And since marriage is permanent and binding, it's natural to panic at the thought you could be settling for less than God's best.

If you do suffer serious anxiety about committing to marry, take heart that this fear is understandable, given the dynamics of our age. The good news is that your fear doesn't have to control your life. With time and patience, you can tame commitment anxiety and break its grip. And in the process, you can find the confidence to go ahead with a good opportunity to marry even though some fears and doubts remain.

Part of the healing process involves learning to control the emo-tion of fear itself. You're dealing with runaway emotions that need to be calmed. There are steps you can take to do this, and you have far greater control over your panicky feelings than you probably realize. More on that in a moment.

First, though, I want to suggest some changes in perspective that can greatly reduce your vulnerability to commitment fear. You need the confidence to marry someone with whom you're well matched, even though you haven't met every possible candidate, even though God hasn't given you a special sign, even though "all the facts aren't yet in." Here are five perspectives that can help you turn that corner.

   1. Don't count on God giving you unusual guidance or perfect certainty about whether to marry. Part of what stokes our angst as

Christians is the assumption that, if God wants us to marry, he has one perfect, ideal partner for us, out there somewhere among the vast multitude of humanity. And if that is true, it seems reasonable he will clearly indicate when we've found this person, leaving us with no doubt. If there's ever a time when we should expect special or dramatic guidance from God, it's about this monumental choice we have to make. So we assume.

Scripture, though, cautions us against expecting special guidance from God for any decision, but urges us to take prudent, prayerful responsibility for our major choices. To this end Paul tells us that we who follow Christ "have the mind of Christ" (1 Cor 2:16). Through taking responsibility for our decisions, we grow in ways that wouldn't be possible if God always made it easy for us through direct guidance.

Even in a decision as far-reaching as marriage, Scripture never counsels us to wait for special guidance from God before taking the leap. Rather, Paul declares, "since there is so much immorality, each man should have his own wife and each woman her own husband" (1 Cor 7:2 RSV). Paul's admonition in the Greek literally reads, "Let each man have his own wife, and let each woman have her own husband." In this verse, and throughout his lengthy counsel on deciding about marriage in 1 Corinthians 7, Paul urges readers to take responsibility for their lives. He gives guidelines for choosing marriage or singleness and for deciding whether to marry when an opportunity is present. In all of his emphasis upon deciding responsibly about marriage, Paul says nothing about waiting for special guidance before going ahead. Instead, he advises the person who needs marriage to avail themselves of a good opportunity.

The fact that God wants us to take responsibility for our choices comes as welcome relief to those of us who are tied up in knots looking for unreasonable guidance. We're not expected to wait for perfect certainty about God's will but are free to take initiative. Far from forcing God's hand by doing so, we're fulfilling his intention that we become responsible decision makers. If we pray earnestly that our choices reflect his will, we may trust that he will guide us in his will as we make practical decisions.

2. *Look for a suitable, not perfect, partner.* While Paul says nothing about waiting for special guidance in seeking marriage, he also says nothing about looking for the perfect spouse. He obviously wants Christians to use good judgment in choosing whom they'll marry. But never in his teaching on the marriage decision in 1 Corinthians 7 does he suggest that we should wait until all of our ideals are met before deciding to marry someone.

I find it particularly intriguing that Paul simply assumes his Corinthian readers can find someone appropriate to marry. Their church was only about five years old at this time, and it had many problems. It wasn't likely a huge congregation, and the pool of potential marriage candidates was certainly small. In spite of these limitations, Paul doesn't counsel his readers to go on a search for the ideal mate or even to look outside of their church. He seems to assume that many of them, at least, can find a good opportunity within the Corinthian church itself.

Did Paul believe that God has one ideal choice for each person he wants married? If pressed, he would probably have answered yes, given his emphasis on predestination. Yet Paul never recommends that we should *dwell* on this thought in our search for a partner. His counsel on the practical level can best be summarized not as, "God has one perfect spouse for you," but, "God will help you to find someone *suitable* to marry."

This is one of the most critical shifts in perspective we need to make in seeking marriage. If we're caught up in the belief that God has one perfect mate for us, we're likely to assume that this person—and the relationship—must *be* perfect. If we think, rather, in terms of finding a suitable partner, we're much more likely to see the marriage potential in a relationship with someone who, like ourselves, falls short of perfect.

Beyond the marriage decision, it helps to aim for suitable rather than perfect choices in all of our decisions. Thinking this way allows us to maintain good standards of judgment without being paralyzed by impossible ideals. Regarding work and career, for instance, Scripture never suggests we can find a perfect job. Our career can provide considerable fulfillment, and the Bible encourages us to take pleasure in our work (Eccl 3:13; 5:18-20). Yet a certain burden is always involved in work as well (Gen 3:17-19). We cannot escape this dynamic tension, even in the best job.

3. Confidence in providence. Learning to think in terms of finding suitable opportunities is not our only need, though. We also need to be able to recognize these special opportunities when they occur. We who fear commitment usually need to become much more alert to the open doors God provides.

Nothing helps more to increase our awareness of them than a strong conviction about the role of God's providence in our lives. Scripture teaches that God is working continuously to provide us with good opportunities that offer solutions to many of the needs we face. We need to believe this as a matter of faith.

Subtle differences in how I think about God's providence in my life, though, can strongly affect whether I recognize the opportunities he presents or am oblivious to them. My belief that he has a perfect plan for me, for instance, may lead me to think that choices I make must *be* perfect. In fact, this conviction should lead me to the opposite conclusion. It should help me realize that he is providing excellent opportunities through situations that appear less than perfect from my standpoint. It should inspire me to see his best in my imperfect circumstances.

The fact that God is actively working out his plan in my life, in other words, means that many of the opportunities I face are indeed golden ones. To wait indefinitely for more ideal circumstances before committing myself can show a lack of faith.

While the theme of God presenting good opportunities through imperfect circumstances permeates Scripture, it is especially clear in Jeremiah 29. Here we find one of the Bible's most treasured statements about God's providential role in our lives: "For I know the plans I have for you, says the LORD, plans for welfare and not for evil, to give you a future and a hope" (v 11 RSV). God assures us he is taking profound initiative to work out an incomparable plan for each of us.

But when we recall this verse, we seldom consider the context in which it occurs. The Israelites have been deported to Babylon and are severely depressed over leaving their homeland. They see no good whatever in their current situation and are reluctant to make any long-term commitments in it. Yet Jeremiah instructs them,

> This is what the LORD Almighty, the God of Israel, says to all those I carried into exile from Jerusalem to Babylon: "Build houses and settle down; plant gardens and eat what they produce. Marry and have sons and daughters; find wives for your sons and give your daughters in marriage, so that they too may have sons and daughters. Increase in number there; do not decrease" (Jer 29:4-6).

It is *following* this exhortation to take initiative to rebuild their lives that God then declares, "I know the plans I have for you . . . ."

Because he has good plans for them, God says, the Israelites should see his best in their present *imperfect* situation. They shouldn't wait for more ideal circumstances before taking steps to meet their vital needs. And God notes three major areas where the commitment-fearful Israelites should take initiative:

• *to find suitable living situations* ("build houses and settle down")

• *to find work* ("plant gardens and eat what they produce"—a symbolic way of saying "be gainfully employed")

• *to find marriage and family life* ("marry and have sons and daughters")

Strongly implicit in God's counsel to the Israelites is that he is *providing* good opportunities for them in each of these areas. Yet they won't find them by being idle or skittish about commitment. They must take earnest initiative to discover the best God has for them.

We who fear commitment should consider this passage and its

implications often. It suggests the need for a fundamental paradigm shift in the way we approach our decisions. Rather than insist that a situation must prove itself flawless before we commit ourselves, we should assume that a good opportunity is very possibly one we should choose. Of course we should use good judgment and weigh each option carefully. But we shouldn't be too quick to dismiss an opportunity because it fails to meet all of our ideals. Appreciating God's providential role in our lives should increase our conviction that an open door may be his answer to our needs.

This perspective is especially critical in deciding whether to marry, and can make a huge difference in finding the confidence to seize a good opportunity. Take a typical relationship situation. Alice and Jon have dated seriously for three years and have a deep, caring relationship. Both are mature Christians in their late twenties, and each personally wants to be married rather than remain single. Yet even though they are very much attracted to each other, they cannot resolve whether to marry. Alice worries whether Jon will perfectly meet all of her needs, and Jon wants a clear sign from God before going ahead.

Jon and Alice should put the burden of proof upon why they *shouldn't* marry, however, rather than upon why they should. Apart from a compelling reason, in other words, they should choose to get married. The fact that God has allowed them to tie up several years of their adult lives in a serious romantic relationship is itself a compelling reason to consider marriage, particularly given their level of personal need and the fact that neither they nor their friends see any red flags indicating major problems.

In deciding to marry, then, you should put the emphasis upon giving *reasonable* time to getting to know each other and exploring the option of marrying, and upon having reasonable evidence you two are well matched and are both ready to marry. If you have met this criteria, then it's reasonable to believe in faith that God has shown you providentially you should get married. As an added caution, it's reasonable to ask God to give you a compelling reason if you shouldn't marry, and to assume that if no such reason emerges, you should go ahead.

4. Don't expect perfect peace in advance of your decision. Complicating the matter for many Christians, though, is an unfortunate notion about Christ's peace. Many assume that if God is leading you to do something, you'll experience perfect peace. This is usually thought to mean that no fears or doubts will intrude; if you have any misgivings at all about taking the step, then God is warning you not to go ahead.

While Scripture teaches that Christ gives peace to those who follow him, it never guarantees that we will *feel* peaceful as we begin to take a new direction. God doesn't overrule our psyche. The peace that he gives, rather, enables us to *transcend* our fears— to move ahead in spite of many hesitations. We may feel a mixture of peace and fear at the same time, especially in the early stages of a major life change. Many of us are so constituted psychologically that we simply cannot feel peaceful *in advance* of such a change, but after we have fully followed through. Reaching our destination is vital to experiencing Christ's peace and opening ourselves to the full blessings of God.

Indeed, faith *often* involves the resolve to move ahead in spite of fear. This is as true for the decision to marry as for any other. You can make some progress mastering your fear through the steps I'm suggesting. But in the end, it's critical that you don't allow commitment fear to prevent you from going ahead and marrying. Far too many people who fear commitment bail out of their engagement in order to get relief. Yet it's getting married that brings the truest and most important relief. Once you've made your vows and the wedding is over, once you know your commitment is final and there's no turning back, then your psyche begins to work for you in a new and most welcome way. Most who fear commitment find that from this point on the peace that had eluded them is now strongly present. Indeed, commitment itself is the single most important step toward healing the fear of commitment.

Is it possible, though, that anxiety about marrying might signal legitimate reasons not to go ahead? Absolutely. Anxiety that surfaces after confidently committing to marry can indicate certain issues with your partner or the relationship that you haven't recognized clearly before now. You should carefully examine why you're afraid, and whether your fear indicates possible problems you should honestly face. But here the important thing is, again, to be reasonable. Can you identify at least one compelling reason you shouldn't marry, which your fears have helped you recognize? If so, then fear has been your ally. It has helped you recognize a reservation you may have repressed, ignored or just not recognized till now. Take your fear seriously then. Break the engagement.

Don't take reservations seriously, though, that are merely vague. Nor if they're related to minor annoyances with the other, exaggerated concern of the marriage failing, fears of being locked in, or worries that someone might be out there somewhere who's better suited for you. You're suffering unhealthy commitment anxiety in these cases. Do what you can to calm it. But don't let it keep you from marrying.

5. *Avoid fatalistic thinking.* In addition, avoid ruminations like, "this marriage could be destined to fail." To muse like that is to think like a victim, and not like the proactive person God wishes you to be. The marriage itself is neither destined to fair or succeed, but to a large extent will be what you and your partner make of it. If you both are supportive, compassionate people, dedicated to building a happy, thriving marriage, then you have the ability to make that marriage the best it can possibly be. With God's help, of course! But God gives you this capacity, and wants you to think of your marriage as a ship that you can steer in any direction you choose.

Counteract any fear that the marriage might be fated to fail with the reminder that God enables you to do all the things that will make the marriage strong. And commitment is what positions you to use this ability to full advantage.

These five perspectives will help you break the obsessive

thinking that's at the heart of commitment anxiety. You have a basis to be decisive, to go ahead and take the plunge and marry when a good opportunity beckons, and not to feel you're condemned to an endless search for the perfect mate. Remind yourself, too, that life is finite, and opportunities don't present themselves for ever. If you're mature enough to be married, and you long to be, then you should take a good opportunity now.

Breaking the Panic Cycle

Changing the way you think about the marriage commitment may be all you have to do to eliminate commitment anxiety. Embracing these five outlooks we've just considered may quell your fears enough to enable you to commit to marry with confidence. That's the best-case scenario.

Yet because commitment anxiety is so often at a phobic level, you may be dealing with runaway emotions as well, which have taken on a life of their own. And so to master your fear, you need to approach it on its own turf. Your anxiety isn't fueled solely by how you think, but also by certain physical reactions triggered by your fear, which in turn make you more afraid, creating a vicious cycle. It helps greatly to understand this process, and then to take certain steps to counteract it. Because the emotion of fear is so closely connected to physical reactions, altering these responses can diminish the feeling of fear significantly. Mental discipline helps as well, particularly making a determined effort to halt obsessive thinking the moment it starts. Here are some steps I suggest in *Overcoming Shyness* that are commonly recognized by phobia therapists as effective in combating the onset of fear.[2]

• *Practice abdominal breathing.* When we're stressed, our need for oxygen increases. Typically, we breathe more intensively but into our chests. This "thoracic" breathing results in part from our esteem for the military posture—"stomach in, chest out!" Yet in this position our lungs are not able to expand to receive their full capacity of air. The result is that we feel the need to breathe more quickly, and hyperventilation may occur. When under stress, we need to counter our natural tendency toward chest breathing. Let your stomach relax (and hang out if necessary!), then breathe slowly and deeply into it. Hold your breath for several seconds, then slowly let it out. The tranquilizing effect is remarkable. Continue doing this until your sense of control returns.

• *Relax muscles you tend to tense.* The next time you feel panic coming on, make a point of noticing your muscular responses. Do you clench your hands? Cross your legs tightly? Fold your arms? Tighten your stomach muscles? Push your toes together? Many of us who, like myself, have a frontal bite, clench our teeth. All these reactions increase our stress levels. The clenched jaw, in fact, can produce a number of other unfortunate side effects, including dizziness, distortion in the ear, migraines and facial pain.

Learn to identify your muscular reactions under stress, and then make a conscious effort to counter your natural inclinations. Practice relaxing your muscles when you feel tense. Open your hands and let them hang loosely. Let your jaw hang limp. Resist the temptation to cross your legs or clamp them together. When relaxing the muscles is combined with proper breathing, the physical effects of stress and panic are greatly reduced. As a phobic flyer, I can attest that these simple techniques have done wonders for reducing my uneasiness when airborne. They have helped reduce my anxiety in numerous public speaking situations as well. All of us can experience considerably greater control over our anxiety responses when we follow these practices.

• *Follow a healthy routine of rest, eating, exercise and general management of your time.* Also, take sensible steps to eat properly, get the rest and exercise you need, and manage your time carefully. In general, anything that contributes to your physical well-being helps to reduce your general stress level. Like many people, I find that my appetite diminishes when I'm anxious or fearful. At the same time, when I neglect my normal eating habits, my vulnerability to being anxious increases. If I'm feeling nervous about a trip or a talk, I think of eating as an act of discipline (at other times it's a wonderful celebration, but not now). I go ahead and eat a normal meal, even though I'm not particularly eager to do so. Again and again, I find the simple step of keeping food in my stomach reduces stress.

Here an experience of the prophet Elijah is instructive. After an exhausting encounter with the prophets of Baal, detailed in 1 Kings 18, he panicked upon receiving a veiled threat on his life from Queen Jezebel. He retreated to a solitary spot in the desert and prayed that God would take his life (1 Ki 19:1-8). At this point God helped him in two ways. He sent an angel to make food for him. And he enabled him to sleep peacefully. After several days of such rest and relaxation, his fear subsided and his motivation returned. "And he arose, and ate and drank, and went in the strength of that food forty days and forty nights to Horeb the mount of God" (v 8 RSV).

In this case, God healed a man who was severely traumatized by ministering to his physical needs. The lesson of this incident for each of us is clear: we can reduce our own vulnerability to fear by the way we manage our physical life.

• *Practice thought-stopping*. Finally, we need to take a bold step of mental discipline to thwart obsessive thinking. Specialists who work with phobia sufferers recommend the practice of "thought-stopping."

When an unreasonable fear comes to mind, immediately yell internally (or externally, if no one is around), "STOP!!!" It may help to picture a policeman holding up a large stop sign, blowing his whistle incessantly and commanding you to halt. Be absolutely consistent in doing this every time an irrational thought troubles you. Insist that it cease and desist. Then immediately replace the fearful thought with a pleasant one. Think of a situation that you find relaxing or encouraging. Remind yourself, too, of God's absolute care for you, his desire for your very best, his forgiveness and his complete acceptance of your feelings.

The important thing, specialists point out, is being consistent and persistent in this response. Over time, when combined with other practices I'm suggesting, thought-stopping helps significantly to change patterns of phobic thinking.

These steps will help us greatly to reduce crippling anxiety about commitment, and other phobic reactions as well. If we are serious about conquering chronic commitment fear, we must recognize that our learned emotional reactions are part of the problem. We have developed a *habit* of fearing commitment. Fortunately, habits can be broken. We never have to be the victim of runaway emotions. God has given us much greater ability to defuse the emotion of fear than we normally realize. We are even capable of reversing our instinctive responses to phobic situations.

We should review these stress management techniques often and regard every onset of fear as an opportunity to put them into practice. With practice and persistence, they will enable us to break the cycle of panic and regain emotional control. As an effective response to the emotion of fear becomes part of our lifestyle, our other efforts to overcome commitment fear will bear much greater success.

10

Feeling Like a Fake

T*aking a new direction with our life not only means fighting* through certain fears to get there, but also growing comfortable with our new role once we've in it. Turning the page successfully means embracing a new identity. We're revising our concept of who we are to some degree—in some cases radically. Growing into our new identity can take time, and our new role may not feel fully natural at first. Many of us find this process of reinventing ourselves exhilarating, fueling our life with purpose and adventure. We're thrilled at discovering a new reason why God has placed us on this earth, and joyfully rise to all the unfamiliarity of this occasion.

For others, the reinventing process is more painful, and they're dogged with a sense of inauthenticity. Even when a new role fits them well—even when it truly reflects God's best intentions for their life—they feel uncomfortable taking it on, even fraudulent. They don't feel qualified for what they have to do, nor deserving of any praise for it. Others surely view them as a fake, they fear, or will soon discover that they are.

These impostor feelings can be deeply demoralizing to some people, even as they successfully pursue a new venture, and may cause them to bail out unnecessarily. It's important that we be prepared for the self-doubt and false guilt that can accompany the effort to reinvent ourselves, and know how to respond to it. Here are some examples of how serious the problem is for some, plus some further discussion of the problem, from my *Overcoming Shyness*.[1]

• Richard pastors a Midwestern community church that he helped to found eight years ago. During this time, the fledgling congregation has grown to several hundred members and features a dynamic ministry. Richard was a successful businessman in the community before changing his vocation to pastoral ministry. Inside he still *feels* more like a businessman than a pastor. Almost weekly he becomes frustrated as he struggles to formulate a meaningful sermon for his people, a task that continues to feel unnatural to him. He worries that his attitude falls short of the serenity that should characterize a pastor. The fact that he has to work so hard at producing an effective sermon convinces him, too, that his faith isn't as strong as it should be.

Overall, Richard still feels like a fish out of water in his pastoral identity, even after eight years of fruitful ministry. He is considering leaving the pastorate altogether and even confessing to his congregation that he has been play-acting to a large extent these past eight years.

Ironically, his congregation is extremely pleased with his ministry, and especially with the depth of his preaching. No one seems the least bit concerned that there might be some dichotomy between his public and private images.

• Sheryl is a corporation lawyer in Atlanta. Though her work is esteemed by her colleagues, she finds it hard to reconcile her successful white-collar image with her poor rural upbringing. In her self-image, she still sees herself as a poor farm girl. The first in her family to finish college, let alone grad school, she continues to feel that she's out of her element. She worries that others will see her as a fake or that something will happen to expose her to the world as incompetent.

• Betsy and Henry have dated for three years. They have a supportive, compassionate relationship. They have talked often and enthusiastically about marriage, and Henry is convinced Betsy would be ideal for him. Betsy, though, sometimes feels that she is just going through the motions in their relationship—and that worries her. There are times when she simply doesn't feel supportive of Henry, and times when the romantic sizzle doesn't seem as strong as it should be. Though on one level Betsy wants to be married, she wonders if she is really cut out for a romantic relationship. Sometimes the role seems alien to her independent nature.

• Jason is the father of three children, ages nine, six and four. Those who know him regard him as an excellent parent, and he indeed makes a noble effort to give his kids the attention they need. Yet he confesses that the task of parenting still feels like "too much, too soon" for him. He doesn't feel like a parent but more like a kid at heart. *His* parents—they are the real parents. The role of parent seems distant from how he thinks of himself.

Richard, Sheryl, Betsy and Jason each suffer from an attitude of self-judgment which psychologist Joan Harvey terms the "impostor phenomenon." In *If I'm So Successful, Why Do I Feel Like a Fake?*[2] she describes the plight of numerous individuals who have achieved success in various areas yet are plagued with fear they're not truly qualified for the positions or status they've attained. They worry that others have been fooled, duped into thinking they're more capable than they really are. They attribute their success to some factor other than true ability: luck, availability, charm, personality, hard work, parental influence, tokenism or an employer's need to fill a quota. They look upon themselves as frauds, and live in fear of others' discovering their true colors. These are people, Harvey stresses, who are not genuine impostors but are adept in their areas of accomplishment; still, they're obsessed with fears of being incompetent.

We who are shy almost always struggle with impostor feelings when we achieve success, as well as when we make any effort to change our behavior or improve our lives. Our tendency to analyze and our heightened fear of how people will judge us make us prone to worry that others will think we're fraudulent. Often, too, we're inordinately conscious of mixed motives, and fear that God is displeased with us.

Even if you're not shy, though, you may still feel fraudulent after making a major life change. If you tend to be hard on yourself and self-condemning by nature, you'll probably find it difficult to embrace a new identity. Reinventing yourself feels like a violation of who you really are.

Roles and Ideals

One of the factors that make us subject to impostor feelings, Harvey notes, is that we have to take on roles in life—roles that sometimes don't fit perfectly with the self-image we've long held. Some find assuming *any* role painfully uncomfortable. They are so concerned with being authentic and true to their inner self that any change in outward identity seems unnatural. An example is someone who always feels inauthentic wearing different modes of dress and so wears the same apparel for formal and informal occasions alike.

Others feel comfortable in some roles but uneasy with others, even with some roles that others believe fit them quite well. This is true for each of the four individuals mentioned above. They are trying to accommodate themselves to roles that they fear don't fully reflect their authentic personhood or potential. The result is a feeling of fraudulence, which drains their energy and makes them doubt they are where God really wants them.

Concern among psychologists with the challenge of accommodating ourselves to roles isn't new. Christian psychiatrist Paul Tournier wrote a groundbreaking and probing book on the subject in 1957, titled *The Meaning of Persons*.[3] Tournier notes that life requires us to take on a number of "personas," or "personages," which can never perfectly reflect our true inner self. Anxiety and guilt over the fear of deceiving others often result. While Tournier doesn't use the term "impostor phenomenon," which was coined in the 1970s by Harvey, his concerns are similar to hers in many ways.

As Christians, we're especially vulnerable to feeling fraudulent in new roles, given our acute awareness of the inner sinful nature and the critical need for truthfulness in everything we do. "Thou desirest truth in the inward being," David declares in Psalm 51:6 (RSV). It can seem that assuming any role forces us to appear to the world contrary to how we really are—and thus to violate the biblical requirement for thoroughgoing honesty.

Add to this the sheer number of roles we *have* to assume in any short period of time. In the past week alone I've taken on the roles of teacher, pastor, counselor, writer, song leader, student, husband, father, son, son-in-law, shopper, homemaker, letter writer, customer, friend, neighbor, restaurant patron, driver, businessperson (negotiating for yard work), computer hack (looking into equipment needed for the ministry), musical performer (planning for a presentation by our family), and member of a congregation (sitting through a worship service)— just to mention the ones that come to mind quickly. I'm sure your situation is no different; you find yourself assuming numerous roles not only in a typical week but in a typical day. For the sensitive, thinking Christian, there's a constant struggle in reconciling who you really are with how you must appear to others.

Adjusting Our Self-Image
Fortunately, both Harvey and Tournier have redemptive advice to offer for this struggle. Harvey stresses that we need to redefine our concept of the self. We're too inclined to think of ourselves in terms of one facet of our life or personality. "I'm a homemaker." Or, "I'm an accountant." Or, "I'm an artist." Instead, Harvey argues, we should come to see ourselves as *multidimensional,* or *multifaceted.* We need to learn to think of ourselves in terms of our total mix of

roles and functions, to become comfortable identifying with any of them and with moving in and out of each of them as the situation requires. This is not a denial of our authentic self, but simply a different way of understanding what the human self actually is.

Harvey warns, too, that we must be careful not to fall into an idealized self-image as we take on different roles. Too often, when we rate ourselves as fraudulent in a certain role, we're judging ourselves by an unrealistic standard that in reality no one could live up to. When a woman like Betsy fears she is being inauthentic in a relationship because her romantic feelings vary at times, she misses the fact that these feelings are *never* consistent. There is always an ebb and flow to romantic emotions, even in the best relationships— even in a good marriage. The important thing is to look at the overall pattern of feelings over time.

Harvey also makes the helpful observation that impostor feelings are most likely to strike when we take on a new role. The shy person, for example, who decides to make a concerted effort to be more personable and assertive will at first feel he is being less than authentic in his manner of relating to others. Yet eventually his new approach to people starts to feel natural; he begins to own his new behavior and stops feeling he is merely playing a role, just as the skills of tennis or driving a car become second nature when practiced enough.

Tournier also stresses that we need to redefine how we think of the self and what it means to be an authentic person. While we each have a distinctive inner personhood, we cannot strip away the outward personas—like peeling off the outer layers of an onion—and expect to finally discover the true inner core of the self. Indeed, our personhood is reflected *through* the roles we take on, and cannot be understood apart from them. The key is to choose those personas that best reflect the individual we truly are. Tournier notes,

> We must resign ourselves to this indissoluble connection between . . . the person and its personages. For we are not only one personage throughout our lives; we are innumerable personages.

At each new encounter we show ourselves different; with one
friend we are the serious thinker; with another, the wag; we
change our demeanor to suit each new situation. We are even
many personages at once. . . .

The tension that always exists between the person and the
personage is one of the conditions of our life, and we must accept it. It is part of the nature of man—indeed, it is what makes
him a man.[4]

The Biblical Perspective

When we turn to Scripture, we find interesting support for the conclusions Harvey and Tournier reach, and many further helpful insights besides.

To begin with, the Scriptures stress emphatically that genuine
impostors do exist, and warnings about them permeate the Bible.
(*"Genuine* impostors?" Well, that's the limitation of our language!)
There are numerous examples of false prophets, cagey magicians,
unscrupulous rulers and religious leaders who use the guise of spiritual power to dominate others and further their own selfish ends.
Jesus minces no words in condemning those who are real impostors and in warning us to beware of their menace:

Beware of the teachers of the law. They like to walk around in
flowing robes and love to be greeted in the marketplaces and
have the most important seats in the synagogues and the places
of honor at banquets. They devour widows' houses and for a
show make lengthy prayers. Such men will be punished most
severely. (Lk 20:46-47)

On a less condemning note, there are also examples in Scripture of
individuals who with good intentions entertained taking on roles
that weren't truly suited to their individuality. There's David, who
with all his heart wanted to build the temple for God. Yet God responded that David didn't have the right temperament for the task,
which was to await the reign of his son, Solomon (1 Chron 17:3-12;
22:6-10). Then there is the demon-possessed man from the

Gerasenes whom Jesus healed, who then wanted to travel with Jesus. Jesus replied that, instead, he should return to his hometown and tell everyone there what Jesus had done for him (Lk 8:38-39).

But at the other extreme, the Bible is flooded with examples of individuals who fulfilled God's will by taking on various roles—roles that probably didn't seem fully natural to them at first, and in some cases may never have. There are graphic instances where individuals were clearly uncomfortable with the early stages of a position into which God called them. Moses and Jeremiah were both frightened of public speaking (Ex 4:10-13; Jer 1:6; *terrified* is probably the better term in Moses' case). Gideon suffered from such low self-esteem that he was incredulous at the angel's assertion that he was the right man to lead Israel's army against Midian (Judg 6:15). We infer from the various times that Paul exhorted Timothy not to be afraid, to rekindle his gift or to apply himself to his pastoral task, that Timothy was timid in his pastoral identity and may well have suffered some impostor feelings—this in spite of the fact that he is set forth as the prototype of a good pastor in the New Testament! (See, for instance, 1 Tim 4:12, 14-15; 5:23; 2 Tim 1:7-8; compare 1 Cor 16:10.)

While Moses, Jeremiah and Gideon seem to overcome their initial uneasiness as they became acclimated to their roles, Timothy apparently continued to feel insecure and needed frequent propping up from Paul. It's interesting, though, that God never allowed these men to cave in to the awkwardness they felt; it was never a reason to assume they weren't qualified in God's sight to carry out the role in question.

It's in the same spirit that the New Testament exhorts us in various places to understand our gifts and to give our closest attention to developing and using them. To do so invariably requires assuming some new roles, both as we cultivate a gift and as we apply it in new situations. The chances are good we will experience some impostor feelings as we adjust to new roles and identities that aren't yet natural to us. Yet never does the New Testament tell us to hold back from using our gifts because of these feelings. Rather, we are told emphatically, "If our gift is preaching, let us preach to the limit of our vision. If it is serving others let us concentrate on our service; if it is teaching let us give all we have to our teaching; and if our gift be the stimulating of the faith of others let us set ourselves to it" (Rom 12:6-8 Phillips).

And in case there's any doubt that it's okay for us as Christians to assume different personas in different situations, there's the extreme example of Paul, who proclaimed, "I have become all things to all people so that by all possible means I might save some" (1 Cor 9:22). We have evidence that Paul sometimes felt profoundly uneasy in roles he took on (1 Cor 2:3-5). While he never declared that all believers are required to go to his extreme of adapting to diverse cultural situations, his example does suggest convincingly that *some* modifying of our outward persona not only is permitted but will probably be needed as we seek to realize our full potential for Christ.

Role Playing in Scripture

Perhaps most interesting are those instances in Scripture where individuals actually did play-act in order to make a point or accomplish a goal, fooling others in the process, and yet are not presented as disobedient to God's in doing so. There's the moving episode where Joseph's brothers come to him in Egypt to seek grain during a famine. For some time, Joseph doesn't let on that he's their long-abandoned sibling, but lets them assume he's merely an Egyptian official (Gen 42:1—45:15). Then there's the incident where the prophet Nathan, with a straight face, tells David a fabricated story of a rich man who has stolen a poor man's only possession, a beloved ewe lamb. Nathan uses the story as a creative technique to lead David into brokenness over stealing Bathsheba and arranging for her husband's murder (2 Sam 12:1-12).

Or consider the occasion where David, in order to escape capture by King Achish, pretends to be insane—by foaming at the mouth and scratching at a gate with his hands (1 Sam 21:12-15). Here he acts in an unquestionably deceptive manner, and we might think he had to be violating God's perfect will in doing so. Yet, intriguingly, David wrote Psalm 34 to celebrate the victory God gave him in this incident. And he shows no remorse in that psalm for his play-acting, but implies that through it God enabled him to escape capture by a tyrant. Most stunning, he also declares in that psalm, "Keep your tongue from evil and your lips from telling lies" (v 13). He clearly didn't view feigning madness in this case as inconsistent with living free of deceit.

Of course, the lesson isn't that we have a license to behave deceptively toward others as our general lifestyle. But such behavior isn't fully ruled out by Scripture, either, at least not in certain extreme situations where we might be dealing with a cruel or irrational person, and our own safety or someone else's might be at stake (compare Prov 26:4-5).

But more generally, we can take encouragement from David's example of feigning madness, simply because it's so extreme compared to the typical situations where we judge ourselves as fraudulent. It helps us put these situations into more healthy perspective, and jars us into realizing that our role playing is usually mild by comparison to the play-acting involved in this case. And David apparently wasn't acting contrary to God's will.

Living Boldly

In short, we need to learn to live the Christian life courageously. On the one hand, we need to examine ourselves very honestly, seeking to understand our own hearts and motives as thoroughly as possible. We need to boldly ask God to do whatever necessary to purify our intentions and make our hearts pliable before him. As we come to recognize ways that we're living deceptively or disregarding Christ's standards, we must make the changes needed.

At the same time, we need just as courageously to take bold steps to realize our potential for Christ. We need to seek to understand our gifts and temperament as best as we can, to strive to develop our abilities, and to look for the best opportunities available for investing our gifts and for developing relationships. We should accept that in this process, we'll probably experience some impostor feelings at times, for with personal growth invariably come some journeys through untrodden territory. The fact that we *feel* less than authentic in a role doesn't necessarily mean we're sinning, acting contrary to God's will or violating our true inner self. It may simply be that we're not living up to our own unrealistic standards. There are times when we fail to live up to our own ideals and yet fulfill God's quite well.

Even when our motives are less than perfect, we usually give God the best opportunity to purify them as we stay in motion. It's God's intention that we take on roles, and over the course of our life, many of them. Here we need to make the best choices we can and move on. I agree with Tournier:

> Instead of turning our backs on the outside world and concentrating on our own inner life, where the true nature of the person always eludes us, we must look outward, toward the world, toward our neighbor, toward God. We must boldly undertake the formation of a personage for ourselves, seeking to form it in accordance with our sincerest convictions, so that it will express and show forth the person that we are.[5]

One final point. While Scripture provides us plenty of basis for such bold expressing of ourselves, perhaps the greatest incentive comes from one overriding fact—that of the Incarnation. By choosing to become man in Jesus Christ, God took on a *role.* He assumed an identity that was foreign to who he had been from the foundation of time—first in the form of a baby, and finally in the form of an adult man with all of our humanity (Heb 2:14; 4:15).

The fact of the Incarnation alone should help us feel permission to reinvent ourselves, and to recognize that it may be necessary on occasion. It stunningly symbolizes an aspect of God's design of human life that we're stressing in this book—that most of us need a major life change from time to time, in order to fully realize our potential for Christ and to fully experience the adventures he has in store for us. May the fact that God became human in Christ encourage us likewise to seek those roles and situations where we can best glorify him through being the individual he has made us to be. We may not feel fully comfortable at first in a new role God has for us. But we may rest assured that our discomfort isn't sin, but part of the normal process of growing into a new identity. And here we have every right to say with Paul, "I can do all things in him who strengthens me" (Phil 4:13 RSV).

11

Pulling Up Roots

Among the most cherished possessions Evie and I own is a coin collection. I say "cherished" because part of it was passed on to us by my parents, and part by Evie's. It's what you might call a typical family coin collection: There are some fairly old coins and bills in it—some dating to the nineteenth century. Yet when you meticulously check the value of each piece of currency, you don't find any that will pay off your mortgage. Its total worth is probably under $1,000.

Neither Evie nor I has any interest in collecting coins. Yet we've held on to this collection, as most parents probably would, with the hope of eventually passing it on to our grandchildren (two now and counting).

It finally occurred to me, though, that this long-term goal may not be such a great idea. Inheriting the collection was seamless for Evie and me, because we're both only children. But finding an equitable way to divide such a miscellaneous assortment among several grandkids could be difficult. One of them might want certain coins given to another, and feel treated unfairly. Trying to divide the collection fairly between them could be downright unpleasant—quite the opposite experience you would hope for in bestowing a gift.

Then I thought of an alternative plan: We could sell the collection, and invest the proceeds in a savings account. Over time, that account's value would probably appreciate more than the coin collection would. Then, at some future point, we could take each grandchild to a coin shop and allow each one to spend an even share of that account on whatever coins he or she chooses. No child could possibly feel cheated this way. In fact, this idea seemed like the perfect solution to me intellectually—an ideal win-win arrangement for everyone.

But I haven't been able to bring myself emotionally to carry it out. This collection is part of our family's history, and passed down over several generations. It seems sacrilegious to part with it.

This—in spite of the fact that if you replaced these coins and bills with ones of similar age and value, I wouldn't be able to tell the difference, for I haven't examined this collection in years! I don't have a clue what *specific* items of currency are included in it. Still, it's *our* collection—*our family's* collection. How could I possibly let go of it?

The Endowment Effect

My hesitation to sell the family coin collection reflects a tendency that financial counselors call "the endowment effect." It's our inclination to value something more highly than it's actually worth, simply because we own it. We think of the possession as an extension of ourselves. And even if we would clearly benefit by parting with it, we may hold on to it for nostalgic reasons.

The endowment effect often muddies our thinking in important financial decisions, and hinders serious investing. If you've long held General Motors stock, for instance—even more so if your family has—you may attach sentimental value to it. Never mind if there are countless stock options out there offering a better return. You may find it hard to think of letting go of GM and buying something else.

The term "endowment effect" was coined by risk management specialist Richard Thaler in the early 1970s. As a doctoral student in behavioral finance, Thaler became intrigued with "the disparity between prices for which people were willing to buy and sell the identical items."[1] This fascination led him to devote much of his life to studying how we tend to value things more once we own them.

In one experiment, he and an associate gave Cornell coffee mugs to students at that university, and then told the students to take them home. Later, these students were asked to specify the lowest price for which they would consider selling their mug, and the average was $5.25. Other students were asked what was the highest price they would pay for such a mug, and that average was $2.25.

Thaler conducted many other experiments, all pointing to the same conclusion: "Once something is owned, its owner does not part with it lightly, regardless of what an objective valuation might reveal."[2]

These same tendencies that can cause us to prize certain possessions too highly can cause us to overvalue other attachments in our life as well. We can become too emotionally tied to a relationship, a home, a region where we live, a hobby, a church, a club—as well as to certain features that make up our life, such as our habits, traits, expectations, social status and lifestyle. We are overrating any of these things *if* we find it hard to let go of it when we know we would benefit by doing so.

Inertia

I mention the endowment effect in concluding this book to note that, apart from the fears of failure, success and commitment that can keep us from risking, and the impostor fears that can torture us once we step forward, is the simple fact that we can become too attached to our past. We can grow so attached to a certain situation or feature of our life, and our identity be so rooted in it, that it's hard to let go of it, even if a much better option presents itself.

Everything we've said about the fears and apprehensions that hold us back from God's best options for us can be summarized by saying that *inertia is a subtle but extremely powerful force in our lives*. We first stressed this point in chapter three, but now can appreciate it much more fully. We tend to stay in place, firmly rooted in our past, apart from a strong enough incentive to risk something new.

Breaking the inertia is more challenging than we usually recognize, and that's what, above all, I've been trying to stress in the past section, and earlier in chapter three, when we spoke of self-consistency. If we're not held back by self-consistency, or by fears of failure, success, or commitment, we may still be too attached to our past—that is, too focused on what we have to give up to take our life in a new direction. Most of us are so wired that *some* inertia factor will hinder us when we consider a major life change. Without continuing the discussion indefinitely (and making this book another inertia factor!), I want to conclude by stressing three redemptive actions we can take to fight inertia, and to keep it from being the controlling factor in our destiny. This will allow me to reemphasize the importance of staying alert, which we stressed earlier, and to offer some further counsel as well.

1. Stay Alert
During our lifetime, God gives us a number of opportunities to take our life in a new direction; this is the normal experience for most of us. The frequency of these new beginnings differs for any one of us, and may total a handful to a dozen or more. On occasion, it may include the chance to reinvent ourselves in a major way. *How* God conveys these opportunities to us varies considerably and is never predictable.

Sometimes his prompting is blatant. A friend of mine is an

electrician who, because of certain disabilities, has long had difficulty finding and maintaining a decent job. Tom began to wonder if he should simply try to live contentedly unemployed. But recently a friend left Tom a stunning voice mail, saying he wanted to create a job in his company tailored to Tom's physical condition and availability to work. Tom hesitated to respond, wondering if he was ready for such a new horizon. But in the following days his friend attempted twice more to phone him, leaving more upbeat messages. Tom finally concluded this was a rare golden offering God had brought across his path.

And so it is an opportunity can impress itself on us so obtrusively that we have to try very hard to miss it. This isn't a frequent occurrence for most of us, and it may be once in a lifetime for Tom. But God is good and sometimes makes it easy for us, leaving us only with the question, "Is this too good to be true?"

More typically, a great opportunity presents itself much more subtly. *Some* indication is there—a suggestion—that something good may be in store for us if we act. But it takes keen alertness to see it, and vibrant faith to believe that this glimmer of hope may reflect a compelling possibility for us.

I shared earlier how my grandfather, Milton D. Smith, met Kitty Horton, who became his wife. While on duty one day, this Washington, D.C. patrolman stopped a car for speeding around Dupont Circle. It was likely just one of many traffic stops he made in a typical day. But Kitty, the driver, was slightly flirtatious, and Granddad saw a possibility in this brief encounter. He called on her, a relationship blossomed, and they married.

This is how it works for most of us most of the time. God *doesn't* make it too easy for us, for he knows that would thwart our growth and diminish our sense of adventure. But he does provide an indication that a welcome opportunity may await us if we seize the moment. It's our prompting to get further information and explore the possibility that it's time for an important step of faith.

We must be sharply alert and expectant to perceive God's

indication at such a time. If discouragement is ruling our life, or laziness, we may miss a critical signal, and assume life is simply "business as usual."

It's hard to exaggerate the importance of prayer in gaining this vital alertness. By praying, we put ourselves in communication with God, greatly increasing the chance we'll recognize his prompting. And by the simple but often overlooked step of asking for his guidance, we increase the likelihood we'll receive it.

In the early 1980s, Evie and I felt the need for a new home. While our townhouse would have been adequate under most circumstances, my ministry was operating out of it, and office space wasn't sufficient. Yet the real estate market was the worst in decades, with outlandish mortgage interest rates, around 18%. We couldn't afford to move, and the prospects of selling our present home were nil.

For several months I spent much time studying the market and reading real estate brochures, but only became increasingly discouraged. Finally, it dawned on me that I hadn't spent any serious time praying about the matter. I set aside two hours to pray and seek the Lord's direction, even though it seemed an intrusion into my "busy" schedule. I decided to take a leisurely drive in the country as I prayed, a practice I've often found helpful.

As I meandered around the rural highways of upper Montgomery County, I came upon a street I had never noticed before, even though I thought I knew every nook and cranny of this Maryland county where I've spent most of my life. On that street was a house for sale—one that immediately seemed right for our needs. But it would surely be too expensive. Within a week, the owner accepted a contract from us; the price was considerably below market value. Within another week, our townhouse sold, even though similar homes in our community had been on the market for months without selling.

The lesson isn't that my prayers bent God's mind and constrained him to do something he wouldn't otherwise have wanted to do.

This was not the "health and wealth gospel" at work. What happened during those several hours, I believe, was that God was able to command my attention and show me a way to solve an "impossible" problem. He could just as well have given me grace to accept things as they were. In fact, that has happened far more frequently than the more dramatic sort of answer that came on this occasion. In this case, though, God had a solution to our family's needs, but needed my attention to enlighten me.

Today, 32 years later, we're still living in this house, which has consistently proven remarkably well-suited for us. Yet the inspiration to consider buying it came quickly—in a flash—as I came upon this home unexpectedly while driving. And that serendipitous moment came while I was praying for guidance about this specific need.

While prayer serves many purposes, one of its most important is helping us secure God's guidance. Most of us take a default approach to praying for guidance. We may do so on occasion, but as a footnote to our own efforts to solve our problems. Yet praying for God's direction should be more than an afterthought, and ought to be a serious commitment. Make a habit of devoting some time early each day to asking God for direction during the day ahead, and alertness to his prompting. Then do your best to maintain a spirit of prayer throughout the day—looking to him for guidance and any signal a situation deserves special attention. Then, whenever you sense it may be time to take a new direction or significant step with your life, devote a more substantial period to praying for guidance and openness to God's will—an hour or two, or more. As these practices become habits, you'll find your alertness to God's subtle indications increases, along with your confidence about when it's time for a major life change.

2. Be Courageous
Our second overriding need for avoiding inertia's pull is courage, and we need to constantly strive for it. We've looked at various

hurdles to courage throughout Part Two this book, and have stressed various steps we can take to boost our courage for important steps of faith. But ultimately, our need is simply to *be* courageous. While that may sound oversimplified, I believe each of us understands instinctively what this means. Consider how often the Bible simply tells us to be strong, without providing instructions on how to do it. We understand intuitively what it means to rise to an occasion. It means going ahead and doing what's necessary, even though we're frightened or even terrified. It means letting what's right rule our action, rather than our fears. And the truth is that as we *act* courageously, when a situation requires it, we best position ourselves for God to impart courage to us, and we best open ourselves to his provision and welcome surprises.

Last week I joined an auditorium full of parents at the elementary school where my wife teaches, to watch a musical, which the students had worked on diligently for most of the school year. Afterward, the teacher who directed it read a poem she had written, tributing the students for their effort. She stood without a podium, holding the pages on which the poem—about eight minutes long—was written. Her hands trembled noticeably from stage fright; she was clearly panicked at being the center of attention. But she pressed on anyway, her voice strong, and finished the poem to strong applause. This was courage in clear display—staying the course with what she had to do, in spite of significant fear.

In the same way, and on a grander scale, we're likely to feel panicked at certain times when taking a new direction with our life. We should do everything we can to address these fears, and take every step we know to calm them. But we should also be determined to move ahead in spite of fear, to whatever extent we need to. This is what courage means—it's defined by our action, not our feelings. As Franklin D. Roosevelt expressed it, "Courage is not the absence of fear, but rather the assessment that something else is more important than fear." What we need to understand is that we are *capable* of displaying this courage. Acting courageously is as simple as assuming we can—and as profound. It's a matter of staring fear down, of not letting it have the final word. And it's by acting in courage that we open ourselves to God's strengthening, as well as to some of his greatest blessings we're likely to enjoy in our lifetime.

The Bible constantly stresses the importance of courage, along with the benefits that result. Reflecting on passages that exalt courage can help us find the heart to act boldly, and we should review such passages often. Here's a sampling of the many Scripture presents:

• "Do not be afraid. Stand firm and you will see the deliverance the LORD will bring you today. . . . The LORD will fight for you; you need only to be still" (Ex 14:13-14).

• "Do not be afraid of anyone, for judgment belongs to God" (Deut 1:17).

• "See, the LORD your God has given you the land. Go up and take possession of it as the LORD, the God of your fathers, told you. Do not be afraid; do not be discouraged" (Deut 1:21).

• "The LORD himself goes before you and will be with you; he will never leave you nor forsake you. Do not be afraid; do not be discouraged" (Deut 31:8).

• "The LORD is a stronghold for the oppressed, a stronghold in times of trouble. And those who know thy name put their trust in thee, for thou, O LORD, hast not forsaken those who seek thee" (Ps 9:9-10 RSV).

• "The LORD is my light and my salvation—whom shall I fear? The LORD is the stronghold of my life—of whom shall I be afraid? When the wicked advance against me to devour me, it is my enemies and my foes who will stumble and fall. Though an army besiege me, my heart will not fear; though war break out against me, even then will I be confident" (Ps 27:1-3).

• ". . . thou didst hear my supplications, when I cried to thee for help. Love the LORD, all you his saints! . . . Be strong, and let your heart take courage, all you who wait for the LORD!" (Ps 31:22-24 RSV).

• "I sought the LORD, and he answered me; he delivered me from all my fears. Those who look to him are radiant; their faces are never covered with shame. This poor man called, and the LORD heard him; he saved him out of all his troubles. The angel of the LORD encamps around those who fear him, and he delivers them. Taste and see that the LORD is good; blessed is the one who takes refuge in him. Fear the LORD, you his holy people, for those who fear him lack nothing" (Ps 34:4-9).

• "God is our refuge and strength, an ever-present help in trouble. Therefore we will not fear, though the earth give way and the mountains fall into the heart of the sea, though its waters roar and foam and the mountains quake with their surging. . . . The LORD Almighty is with us, the God of Jacob is our fortress" (Ps 46:1-3, 7).

• "My son, keep sound wisdom and discretion; let them not escape from your sight, and they will be life for your soul and adornment for your neck. Then you will walk on your way securely and your foot will not stumble. If you sit down, you will not be afraid; when you lie down, your sleep will be sweet. Do not be afraid of sudden panic, or of the ruin of the wicked, when it comes; for the LORD will be your confidence and will keep your foot from being caught" (Prov 3:21-26 RSV).

• ". . . fear not, for I am with you, be not dismayed, for I am your God; I will strengthen you, I will help you, I will uphold you with my victorious right hand. . . . For I, the Lord your God, hold your right hand; it is I who say to you, 'Fear not, I will help you'" (Is 41:10, 13 RSV).

• "'For I know the plans I have for you,' declares the LORD, 'plans to prosper you and not to harm you, plans to give you hope and a future'"(Jer 29:11).

• "I called on your name, LORD, from the depths of the pit. You heard my plea: 'Do not close your ears to my cry for relief.' You came near when I called you, and you said, 'Do not fear.' You, Lord, took up my case; you redeemed my life" (Lam 3:55-58).

• "Let the weakling say, 'I am strong!'" (Joel 3:10).

• "Do not let your hearts be troubled and do not be afraid" (Jn14:27).

• ". . . for God did not give us a spirit of timidity but a spirit of power and love and self-control" (2 Tim 1:7 RSV).

• "Do not be anxious about anything, but in every situation, by prayer and petition, with thanksgiving, present your requests to God" (Phil 4:6).

These passages stress emphatically that God enables us to rise to occasions that intimidate us. The most important key to overcoming fear is to act in spite of it, trusting that God will give us strength, along with results that reflect his best intentions for us. That attitude is courage, and it can transform our life and enable us to realize our highest potential for Christ. And when courage is our ally, we're best positioned to break the inertia that keeps us bound, and to achieve the dreams God inspires in us.

Which brings us to the third essential step for resisting inertia's pull, which is . . .

3. Seek Inspiration

Something stunning happens when we want a certain outcome strongly enough. Our fears melt away, or at least take a back seat to our desire. Our psyche doesn't hold on to conflicting feelings well, and the stronger emotion tends to override the weaker. When desire is intense enough, it subdues our fear, propelling us to take the risks needed to realize a cherished goal.

As a young man, I feared flying so badly that I would go to any lengths to avoid the unfriendly skies. When I had to fly, I endured the trip with white knuckles, and knees that shook off the Richter scale.

Yet on one memorable occasion, I flew without fear. No one was more surprised than I was.

When I awoke that morning, in March 1974, I wasn't expecting to fly anywhere. I was managing Sons of Thunder at the time. Yet I was no longer playing guitar with this band, which I had performed with for over six years. I had requested this change, being newly married, and hoping for a more stable family life than band travels typically allowed.

I did miss performing. On this day I missed it especially, for SOT was scheduled to play at Wheaton College that evening. We felt high honored by this invitation. Many of the pastors and Christian leaders we most respected were graduates of Wheaton, and many from our own church had attended there.

Throughout the day, I felt chagrined over missing this cherished opportunity. I kept wishing I could walk on stage with the band that evening. Then late that afternoon, it happened, against the odds. SOT's music director, Tom Willett, phoned to say that the band's present guitarist was delayed on the road and wouldn't be able to make the concert. Was there any chance I could fly to Chicago and fill in? A flight was leaving Washington at 7:30, he explained, and the concert could be delayed until 9:30. With the hour gained flying west, I would hopefully arrive in time.

Ecstatic, I told Tom I would do it if I could possibly make the flight. That would be no small challenge. It was already past 5:00, and we lived in a remote Maryland town, over an hour's drive from Virginia's National Airport. Evie and I scrambled to pack, drove frantically to the airport, then waited less than patiently in the ticket line. We walked onto the plane at 7:29.

When the cabin doors slammed shut, just after we took our seats, I felt not the usual surge of panic, but elation. I was going to make the concert! For the next two hours, as the plane hurtled through the jet stream and bounced over air pockets, I felt no dread. I was too eager to enjoy the benefits this passage through the firmament would bring, too caught up in the adventure of beating the odds. There was simply no room in my psyche for fear that evening.

And yes, my adventure has the happiest ending. I did make the concert, which came off well and was an important milestone for us.

This story, which I first shared in *The Yes Anxiety*,[3] is a parable to life on the broadest level. When our desire for a certain new horizon is strong enough, it suppresses our fears or even eliminates them. At worst, it transforms them into excitement and the sense that we're embarking on a grand pursuit.

When we first muse about taking a new direction with our life, it's easy to feel strongly inspired. Our inspiration often runs at full throttle then, when it's all still fantasy, and we haven't committed ourselves or taken any steps that have backfired. As we begin to weigh the option more seriously, or start to move ahead, we're vulnerable to all the fears and apprehensions we've discussed. Our excitement may increasingly fade, and we may forget why we chose this new path to begin with. In the worst case, we may cave in to fear, and bail out of a dream that would succeed for us wonderfully if we just pressed on.

One of our greatest needs in pursuing a new dream is to do whatever needed to keep our inspiration strong. Regardless of the fears or concerns that dog us, if we want the outcome strongly enough, we'll forge ahead. There are several time-honored steps we can take to rekindle our inspiration when it wanes, and ensure it stays potent enough to move us toward our goal.

• *Seek the encouragement of others.* We've stressed our need for others' encouragement throughout this book, but it will help to look at its role once again. God has made us to be social creatures—that may seem only too obvious. But part of this reality is that we absorb the feelings of those around us, including how they feel about us and the goals we choose to pursue. Simply being in the presence of someone who is enthusiastic about a dream of ours, and believes it's right for us, can stir our motivation and give us the heart we need to stay on course. Even a brief encounter with such a person can make a world of difference.

Halfway through the doctor of ministry program at Fuller Theological Seminary, I lost my zeal. My pastoral heartstrings tugged at me; I wanted to get out of academia and back into people-centered ministry. I came close to quitting.

On Evie's advice, I decided to seek counsel from the dean of students. When I walked into his office the next morning, he received me warmly and spoke with me at length, even though I hadn't made an appointment. After I explained my dilemma, he offered some simple advice: Since I had come this far in the program, it was a minimal sacrifice to continue. Besides, the long-range benefits of finishing the degree well outweighed the momentary relief of getting out. That was just about the sum and total of his counsel.

But it hit a receptive chord. Most of all, his positive, affirming spirit was reassuring; I felt he believed in me and in my potential to benefit from the program. By the end of our meeting, my motivation had begun to return. I'm now eternally grateful to this man for his advice and encouragement. Staying with the program gave me the background to write my first book, and the degree has opened numerous doors of ministry. In this case, God used a man—one individual—to keep me from a regrettable course of action. Were it not for his counsel, I likely would have bailed out.

What's most interesting, though, is that my remarkable change of heart came through a single session with this man, and not extended therapy. When I walked into his office, I was ready to resign the program; when I left, I was inspired to continue, and that fire stayed strong enough to propel me to finish. Being in his presence for just a few minutes recharged my motivation, almost as though there were a direct emotional tap between us.

Of course, our need for others' encouragement varies, depending on the goal we're pursuing and the challenges we face. You may need more frequent or substantial reassurance than I did, to stay the course toward your dream. I share this story from my past simply to underscore how much power there is even in a single encounter with someone who believes in you and your possibilities. Whatever your need for support, take advantage of this amazing fact of human nature—that God has created us to rebound through others' encouragement. If fear or doubt threatens to dismantle a dream that's otherwise right for you, seek the encouragement of a supportive friend or acquaintance or counselor. Get yourself into the presence of someone who thinks positively about you and your potential, and let their confidence in you have its contagious effect.

• *Take time to reflect quietly in God's presence.* While God has made us to be social creatures, he has also created us to need private time alone with him, away from other distractions. While such time brings many benefits, one of the most essential is the rekindling of our motivation for the goals God wants us to pursue. This restoring of our passion comes in part from the fact that we're in the presence of God, allowing him an unhindered chance to work within us and fashion our desires according to his will. And it comes also from—simply—*thinking*—from unhindered reflection on the situation where our zeal is lagging. We reason through fears that may be holding us back, and consider why it isn't worth caving in to them. And we focus on the most appealing aspects of our dream, and allow them to dominate our thinking.

Each of us should experiment to find out what our specific needs are for such reflective time, and how to fit it into a daily routine. We should strive to allow for it daily, even if just a few minutes. This practice is easiest for the introvert, who naturally enjoys such private time. But just as the introvert needs to work at being more socially active, the extrovert needs give attention to nurturing his private life. She needs to allow herself to discover the joy and inspiration that can only come through creative solitude.

Ideally, this reverent reflection should be part of a regular devotional time, where we also give attention to prayer and Bible study. The challenge is not to let our devotions get so overloaded with activity that contemplation is neglected. All three of these practices are vital to our spiritual health—prayer, Bible study, and reflection on our life and goals. The third is the most essential, though, for staying motivated about what God wants us to do.

We usually need a more extended period of both prayer and quiet reflection when considering a major life change. If it's right for us to pursue it, our vision for the new option more clearly crystallizes through such a time, and our inspiration grows strong enough to prod us forward.

In early January 1973, I spent a couple of days praying and reflecting in solitude at a camp in Mt. Airy, Maryland. This was when things were growing serious with Evie. At one point during this personal retreat, I had a sudden moment of conviction, where I envisioned Evie and me married, and it simply felt right. As I pondered that inspiration, doubts I had been harboring seemed to melt way. I felt that God was moving me to propose to her, and that on the deepest level, this was what I most wanted to do.

The value of this extended solitude in helping me decide to marry Evie—when my thinking was still unsettled—and in gaining the heart to propose to her, cannot be overstated. If you've been wrestling with whether to take a certain step with your life but can't decide, or if you can't move beyond certain unhealthy fears, try taking a personal retreat. Devote a few hours, an afternoon, a day or more to praying and reflecting carefully about your decision. Choose a location that's pleasant and inspiring to you, and away from normal distractions. You may just find that your resolve accelerates during this time, your vision crystallizes, and the inspiration to follow your dream grows strong enough to be your ally.

There will also likely be times in pursuing any major dream when your passion wanes or fear threatens to halt you. Taking some extended time for prayer and reflection can reignite your inner fire. For the past several decades, I've devoted substantial time most years to writing. Book writing remains my favorite pastime, and I consider it my most important professional calling. On endless occasions, I've recharged my passion for a project by doing nothing more than reflect quietly for an hour or two. One time I recaptured the vision for an abandoned project I had lost the zeal for about a decade before. With renewed enthusiasm, I completed that book in a few months.

Such serendipities with solitude are common for writers. Yet the fire for any dream can rekindle through relaxed contemplation.

If your motivation for a dream is fading, give this private time a chance. Your vision can rejuvenate surprisingly through unhurried, prayerful reflection, especially in a quiet surrounding with normal distractions absent.

• *Read!* One of my most important turning points occurred during my high school twelfth grade year. I had long been a poor student. Since seventh grade, my heart had been tied up in music, and not my studies. I had devoted my time to learning guitar and developing a band, while homework took a back seat. And of course, the effect was reciprocal: without enough outside study, I wasn't prepared for class, and found it hard to focus. My academic history was so miserable that the high school's guidance counselor advised my mom not to waste the money sending me to college.

It didn't help that I found most textbooks uninspiring. I enjoyed other activities far more, like listening to Top-40 radio, watching TV dance shows and practicing guitar. My feelings about my school books were well-captured by an inscription I scrawled in the front of a history text: "If all the world was flooded, and I was about to die, I'd climb upon my history book, because it is so dry."

By my high school senior year, I longed to turn my academic life around. I still found homework distasteful, though, and music continued to be a major distraction. But in January, my American history teacher made me an offer. If I would read a book he recommended, and submit a report on it, he would boost my grade one letter. I accepted the deal, not realizing that my teacher, I'm sure, believed that reading this book would motivate me more broadly. And he was stunningly correct.

We speak of various experiences being "life-changing," and we use the term so loosely. Yet reading *The American Pageant*[4] truly altered the direction of my life at that time, and for all the time that has followed. Thomas A. Bailey, the author, had a way of doing what no other textbook writer had achieved for me: he made his subject *interesting*. His style was relaxed, personal and free from jargon, yet full of passion. He made broad movements in American history understandable and relevant. *The American Pageant* simply worked for me, and drew me in from the start, as a great novel would. Suddenly, a homework assignment was fun, and deeply inspiring.

The reciprocal effect on my overall academic performance was substantial. Through reading this book, I found I could absorb the facts of history much better than I imagined. That success encouraged me to try harder in my other subjects, and suddenly I was taking them all more seriously. And of course, with greater focus, those courses became more interesting, which in turn inspired me to work harder. My grades shot up that final high school semester, and I opted for college.

The state university, which admitted any Maryland student on a trial basis then, was the default option for those with marginal records, and I entered the University of Maryland that fall. I performed well enough there to transfer to the school of my choice, Georgetown University, the following year. I graduated four years later from Georgetown's business college, fifth in my class. From there, it was off to a masters at Wesley Theological Seminary, then a doctor of ministry at Fuller Theological Seminary. For most of the nearly forty years since, my career has focused on teaching and, increasingly, on writing, and this book will be my fifteenth. Yet this trajectory my life has taken began with reading a single book, which inspired me to do what I thought wasn't possible for me—to succeed in academics.

I mention these accomplishments not to commend or exalt myself, but to underscore the profound effect reading can have upon our psyche, and how it can help us find the heart to achieve a dream. Whatever new direction you envision for your life—marriage, a new job or career, a geographical move, learning a new skill, becoming more socially or creatively active in some way—there are books out there that address your interest. The right book can touch your heart deeply, expand your thinking, address questions and doubts, give you a map to follow, and most important, provide the inspiration you need to move forward.

And never in history has it been easier to find that book. The Internet makes it exquisitely easy to explore the options and preview them online. In America, it's hard to a find a book that isn't available for quick delivery in some form, either new or used, and a vast number are available for instant download. Think of these extensive book options as a gift of God, and the right book a hidden treasure that can stoke your motivation for what God wants you to do.

Books on decision making, discovering God's will, finding your niche, realizing your potential, overcoming fear, and, yes, major life change, can be extremely helpful at life's turning points as well. It's to that end that I offer this book, hoping it will make a difference in your life's journey. I hope it has helped inspire you to be all you can be for Christ, and to take the risks necessary for this to happen. I hope that you're feeling greater permission now to dream big, and to feel the pulsebeat of a dream strongly enough that fear takes a holiday. And I hope this book will be a resource you turn to when considering a new venture with your life, or when motivation lags after you take it on.

Whatever the dream that's on your heart at the moment, I wish you wisdom in determining if God is prompting you to take this new direction, or even to reinvent yourself in a significant way. If you do choose to turn this page, I wish you success in reaching your major goals, and courage to move beyond all the unreasonable fears that stand in your way. Most of all, I wish you inspiration from God's Spirit so strong that it transforms any frightening part of your quest into a compelling adventure.

Appendix

Promises and Vows:
Are We Ever Free To Reconsider?

John, *a Boston native, was a recent seminary graduate want-*ing to pastor a Presbyterian church. For several months, none of the options he pursued materialized. Finally, a rural Kansas church showed interest in him and flew him there to candidate. The interview went well. Yet the people expressed frustration to John about their recent experience with pastors. The past five, they explained, had been new seminary grads who stayed only a year or two before moving on to a more prestigious position. They were naturally leery about hiring another young minister, fresh out of training, coming there as his first position. Would John be willing to make a generous time commitment as a condition of his call?

In a fit of idealism, John promised not to leave or seek another church for at least five years. Persuaded of his sincerity, the church invited him to be their pastor. What John didn't know was that their invitation was based more on his promise than his gifts. Several previous candidates who were more fit for this position had been turned down because they were unwilling to make a pledge of time.

After two years, it was plain to John and to many in the church that things weren't working out. John's urban orientation gave him little empathy for the concerns of this rural congregation, and his cerebral preaching style went over most members' heads, few with any college education. There was fault on both sides. The church, as John had come to discover, was largely composed of ten extended families, who were following decades of comfortable inertia by attending church. Church was a convention for them, and few had a passion for spiritual growth.

A church in a Chicago university district approached John about becoming their pastor. John knew this position would much better match his talents. With some trepidation, he broached the question of leaving with his church's five-member session. He confessed ambivalence, in light of the time commitment he had made.

The session responded with equal uncertainty. They agreed his ministry wasn't being well received, and they admitted upfront that he wasn't legally obligated to stay. But they stressed that many would be mortified if he left. The committee who had discovered him would lose face, and the congregation wasn't eager to undergo the grueling search for a new pastor any time soon. John would have to weigh all of these factors and make his own decision.

John finally concluded that since he had committed to five years, he was bound before God to carry out this term, unless fired, and he decided not to move on. From that point on, though, he rarely experienced the vibrant sense of call that had ignited him at first. He felt more like a sacrificial lamb than anything. His effectiveness dwindled even more, and after five years, people were happy for him to leave.

John's predicament at this Kansas church illustrates an issue we sometimes face when considering a new direction for our life. What if taking this new path means violating a promise we've made—to someone, or to a group of people, or to an organization—to devote our life in a different way? And what if the person or people to whom we've given our pledge will not release us? Are we obligated to fulfill our promise, even if we have reason to believe we would be more productive and benefit others more if we broke it?

It can be especially vexing if we've vowed to God to take on a certain responsibility or mission but then find the role doesn't fit us well. Or if we promise him we'll alter our behavior or lifestyle in a certain way, but then are miserable with the change. Do we ever have the freedom to renegotiate such a vow, and to ask God to release us?

Most often, we don't have to wrestle with breaking a promise or vow when we're considering a major life change, and many of us will go through life without ever facing this challenge head-on. But it will be an issue for some of us on occasion, and when it is, it can be troubling to resolve, even tortuous. In this appendix section, I want to look at this matter carefully, and consider whether following Christ may ever require us to act against a promise we have made.

I'll leave untouched here the question of whether it's ever permissible to leave a marriage. The Bible regards the marriage commitment as the most sacred and binding pledge we can make in our lifetime, and in most cases considers it irrevocable. Those occasional times when divorce or remarriage might be permitted for the Christian throw us into questions of law and grace that take us well beyond the scope of this book. I examine these issues in detail in *Should I Get Married?*, and I refer you to that book if you're wrestling with whether to leave your marriage or remarry after a divorce.[1]

Our discussion in this section relates to most other situations where we've made a promise or vow. They include, most obviously, career choices, but also certain lifestyle decisions (a vow of chastity, a promise to a dying spouse not to marry again, a vow of poverty), and occasional avocational choices as well (a pledge to a church or association to take on a certain responsibility). In any of these cases, we have the potential to make a promise that amounts to more than God wishes us to deliver. But what is our responsibility then? Do we best honor God and love others by breaking the promise, or by doubling down and carrying it out?

Can a Promise Become an Idol?

There's a sense within us humans that a promise binds us not only on earth but in heaven. The thought of breaking it can fill us with the same holy fear we feel in ripping up a threatening chain letter, or in acting against another Christian's prophecy. The fear is expressed in early childhood expressions like "cross my heart and hope to die," and is often revealed in impulsive statements we make as adults. When talking with a pastor about a project we were collaborating on, I blurted out, "I would kill myself rather than be disloyal." We can feel this dread even when we know it's not in others' best interests that we fulfill our promise, and even when others are no longer counting on us to carry it out. The promise takes on a compulsive life of its own.

Consider, for instance, the compelling power of a promise made to a dying person. Psychologist Martha Friedman describes one of her patients, Charlie, who promised his dying father he would become a doctor. Later, he realized his temperament fit him far better for social work. Yet that promise, and the plea of his dying dad, went with him and carried the effect of an immutable vow. He survived doing mediocre work in mediocre medical schools and, finally, as a mediocre doctor. Friedman comments, "There is every possibility that his father's dying words may put Charlie—and others—in jeopardy."[2]

The heightened sense of obligation to God that we feel as Christians can make us even more prone than others to thinking of a promise as a divine commission, which must be carried out at the risk of offending God. This is especially true of promises made directly to God himself. And make them we do! What young Christian hasn't, in the euphoria of a retreat or personal devotions, made

some far-reaching and impossible vow? *Lord I promise—*
* *to spend at least an hour-and-a-half daily praying and studying Scripture*
* *never to masturbate again*
* *not to date anymore*
* *to become a missionary*
* *to witness to at least one person every day for the rest of my life*
* *to sleep no more than six hours a night*
* *never to miss another worship service*
* *never to lose my temper again*
* *never to break a commitment to anyone.*

And what Christian hasn't suffered morbid guilt upon finding she lacks the capacity to keep her vow. Many fear they're no longer in fellowship with God. Not a few conclude they can't continue following Christ.

Yet a promise doesn't have to be made directly to God for us to feel it's like a vow binding us before him. Any promise or commitment we make to anyone can invoke this sense of holy fear within us. Giving our word to another person can feel tantamount to giving our pledge to God.

Vowing in the Old Testament

We're not without biblical prototypes for this attitude. It's hard to exaggerate how deadly seriously promises were taken in the Old Testament. These commands in the Pentateuch, for instance, mince no words about one's obligation to fulfill a vow, whether it's made directly to God or to someone else by swearing on God's behalf:

"Do not swear falsely by my name and so profane the name of your God. I am the LORD" (Lev 19:12).

"When a man makes a vow to the LORD or takes an oath to obligate himself by a pledge, he must not break his word but must do everything he said" (Num 30:2).

"If you make a vow to the LORD your God, do not be slow to

pay it, for the LORD your God will certainly demand it of you and you will be guilty of sin. But if you refrain from making a vow, you will not be guilty. Whatever your lips utter you must be sure to do, because you made your vow freely to the LORD your God with your own mouth" (Dt 23:21-23).

When we look at how people in the Old Testament regarded vows they had made, we find two consistent realities. First, a vow or pledge was considered absolutely binding and nonnegotiable, whether one made it to God or to another person. Not to fulfill it was to kindle God's wrath. Second, one even felt bound before God to fulfill a pledge to do something outlandish or grossly unkind. This was true even when one pledged without full knowledge of the facts, or in response to deceptive information. The vow created a mandate of its own that had to be fulfilled.

By disguising himself as his brother Esau, for instance, Jacob secured from his father Isaac the blessing of the first son, to which Esau was entitled. Even after Isaac realized Jacob had deceived him, he refused to revoke the blessing and bestow it on Esau himself. Because he had already pledged it to Jacob, he considered it binding, even though Jacob had obtained it deceptively (Gen 27:1-40). In another similar case, the nation of Gibeon deceived Joshua and the elders of Israel into making a covenant of peace with them, by pretending to be a distant nation. When Israel's leaders discovered Gibeon dwelled nearby, they still felt compelled to uphold the covenant. Interestingly, they felt more obligated before God to honor this pledge to impostors than to carry out his explicit command to destroy the nearby nations (Jos 9).

No one, though, more stunningly demonstrates the uncompromising mandate vows produced than Jephthah. Going into battle, he vows to God, "If you give the Ammonites into my hands, whatever comes out of the door of my house to meet me when I return in triumph from the Ammonites will be the LORD'S, and I will sacrifice it as a burnt offering" (Jg 11:30-31). Returning home victorious, he is greeted at the door by his daughter. Though distraught,

Jephthah never questions his duty to fulfill his vow, even though it requires killing his only child.

Interestingly, his daughter doesn't challenge his obligation either. "'My father,' she replied, 'you have given your word to the LORD. Do to me just as you promised, now that the LORD has avenged you of your enemies, the Ammonites. But grant me this one request. Give me two months to roam the hills and weep with my friends, because I will never marry.'" The passage adds, "After the two months, she returned to her father and he did to her as he had vowed" (Jg 11:36-37, 39).

The New Testament Perspective

When we come to the New Testament, we find a shift in attitude toward vows and promises that's on the one hand striking, but on the other subtle enough to elude us if we're not looking for it. For one thing, we don't see New Testament Christians making the resolute oaths so common in the Old Testament. Paul does make a vow, along with four other Christians, to follow certain Jewish purification rituals for a week (Acts 21:23ff). Paul clearly took this vow for missionary purposes, to persuade the local Jews that he wasn't antagonistic toward their practices. This strategic step in no way implied that he felt the same religious compulsion about vows as the Old Testament Jews. We have no reason to interpret any differently one other reference to Paul fulfilling a vow—in this case to have his hair cut off—in Acts 18:18.

The only New Testament instance paralleling the Old Testament practice of resolute vowing, interestingly, occurs not among followers of Christ, but with Jewish enemies of Christ and Paul. Luke describes the incident in Acts 23: "The next morning some Jews formed a conspiracy and bound themselves with an oath not to eat or drink until they had killed Paul. More than forty men were involved in this plot. They went to the chief priests and elders and said, 'We have taken a solemn oath not to eat anything until we have killed Paul'" (Acts 23:12-14). They did not, of course, succeed in carrying out their pledge. It would be interesting to know if they died of slow starvation! We have no further information on the incident.

At first, the lack of vowing among the early Christians is surprising. The first believers, like the godly heroes of the Old Testament, were zealous people, willing to sacrifice their lives for the cause of Christ. We would expect this fervor to show itself in bold, courageous, and perhaps outrageous declarations of promise, as were common in the Old Testament. Vowing seems to go naturally with religious zeal.

The lack of vowing in the New Testament, though, isn't surprising when considered in light of Jesus' clear teaching against it in the Sermon on the Mount. Here he calls us to an attitude about vowing that is seldom understood or appreciated by modern-day believers: "Again you have heard that it was said to the men of old, 'You shall not swear falsely, but shall perform to the Lord what you have sworn.' But I say to you, Do not swear at all, either by heaven, for it is the throne of God, or by the earth, for it is his footstool, or by Jerusalem, for it is the city of the great King. And do not swear by your head, for you cannot make one hair white or black. Let what you say be simply 'Yes' or 'No'; anything more than this comes from evil" (Mt 5:33-37 RSV).

Many assume that Jesus' intent here is to condemn cursing. But while that's likely part of his purpose, his main concern is to discourage the making of presumptuous promises, or as the NIV renders them in this passage, "oaths." In saying "Do not swear at all," he comes very close to telling us not to make promises of any sort. His point is that making a promise usually implies we believe we have a level of control over our lives that we don't in fact possess. "You cannot make one hair white or black." We don't know our future, and a promise too easily amounts to playing God; we assume our life will definitely take a given course, and so we can confidently pledge that we'll take a certain action.

The book of James also stresses this point clearly. James repeats

Jesus' command not to swear, paraphrasing it: "Above all, my brothers and sisters, do not swear—not by heaven or by earth or by anything else. All you need to say is a simple 'Yes' or 'No.' Otherwise
you will be condemned" (Jas 5:12). Only sentences before, James
declares, "Now listen, you who say, 'Today or tomorrow we will
go to this or that city, spend a year there, carry on business and
make money.' Why, you do not even know what will happen tomorrow. What is your life? You are a mist that appears for a little
while and then vanishes. Instead, you ought to say, 'If it is the Lord's
will, we will live and do this or that.' As it is, you boast in your
arrogant schemes. All such boasting is evil" (Jas 4:13-16).

The connection of thought here is unmistakable. Swearing—
declaring that beyond any question we will do something—amounts
to laying a claim on the future that we don't have. Neither James
nor Jesus means to imply that we should never give any assurance
to others about our intentions. Assurances should be given, but provisionally, with the qualification that God can redirect events if he
wishes. "You ought to say, 'If it is the Lord's will.'"

This is precisely the spirit Jesus counseled when he said, "Let
what you say be simply 'Yes' or 'No.'" He is telling us to keep our
promises simple, and to make them humbly. If someone invites me
to give a talk, I don't have to feel legalistically compelled to respond, "If the Lord wills, I'll do it." But neither should I declare
emphatically that I'll be there. Somehow my answer must reflect a
firm desire to uphold my intention to come (without such assurances, much human activity would be impossible), while stopping
short of locking God in. Through my attitude, if not my language, I
must convey that my life and all events are ultimately under God's
control.

Pride and Promises
This brings us, then, to a vital distinction between the legalistic
spirit unavoidable under the Old Testament law, and the grace-
centered spirit that the New Testament proclaims, which should

define the Christian life. Under the law, I am constantly under the gun to perform deeds that court God's favor. My continual obligation is to keep God pleased with me, and to gain enough merit to deserve his favor and, ultimately, heaven. Making vows and rigidly keeping them naturally fits with this disposition.

But under grace, my responsibility isn't to perform but to *respond*. God has *already* accepted me through Christ's sacrifice; there's nothing I can add to it! My lifelong need remaining is to respond to his moment-by-moment guidance, which I can never second-guess in advance. The making of vows and emphatic promises implies I know more of what God wills for me in the future than in fact I do. It also adds stress and burden to the Spirit-led life that God doesn't intend. Further, and especially critical to understand, it is *sinful* for me as a Christian to make a vow or resolute promise. To do so is prideful, turning spontaneous life under grace back into legalistic performance. This is true whether I make a binding pledge to another person or directly to God himself.

As an example, it's sinful for me to promise God that I'll spend an hour daily praying and studying Scripture. It's healthy for me to choose to have this time for the sake of my spiritual growth, and helpful to plan a specific daily time for it. But I should make this decision, not as an uncompromising pledge to God, but provisionally, with the realization that God may have other intentions for me on some days. This way of thinking contrasts strongly with the vow-type approach some Christian teachers recommend for our personal time with God. Consider the time you plan for devotions as a binding commitment, they insist, and a moral obligation to God. And see that it's fulfilled, regardless of the inconvenience. If you should miss your devotions one day, then atone for it by spending twice the time the next.

This approach, though, turns personal devotions into a legalistic practice to gain God's favor, instead of an activity pursued for our own enrichment. Instead, we should think of our quiet time as a beneficial activity like eating, sleeping, and exercise; these are *priorities*, even strong ones. But if I, say, miss my cup of yogurt for breakfast this morning, I don't feel obliged to eat two cups tomorrow to make up for it! I simply pick up and move on.

But what if you've made a vow to God about personal devotions? Where does that now leave you? Vowing has actually left you in two sinful predicaments. Making the vow itself was sinful. It amounted to taking too much of your life into your own hands. And any failure to carry it out perfectly is also sinful, for as Scripture says, we must not be slack in carrying out a promise to God. What is the answer to this morbid dilemma?

The answer lies in grace and forgiveness. You should pray, confessing to God that you sinned against him by making the vow, and have sinned further by not fulfilling it perfectly. Then, claim the clear promises of grace and forgiveness offered so abundantly in Scripture. Perhaps the most comforting one to recall at this time is given in the words of Paul in Acts 13: "Through [Jesus] forgiveness of sins is proclaimed to you, and by him everyone that believes is freed from everything from which you could not be freed by the law of Moses."

Ask God as well to release you from your vow, and to free you from the bondage in which it has held you.

Then grasp the liberating truth of Scripture: *You are now freed from your vow! It no longer has binding authority over you!* You can forget it completely, as fully as Christ has. You are free now to take healthy steps toward spiritual growth and discipline, not from a need to please God, not from the compulsion of fulfilling a pledge to him, but from a desire to enjoy the unparalleled benefits of a growing relationship with Christ. That's healthy spirituality!

Take these steps to break free from any other life-draining pledge you've made to God. Earnestly ask his forgiveness for presumptuously promising about your future. Ask him to forgive you also for any failure to carry out your promise to the letter. Then ask him to release you from your vow, and from any further obligation to it. Then rejoice in God's merciful forgiveness, and in the freedom he now grants you to make a new beginning. Rejoice as well that you have taken a vital step to free yourself from compulsive, legalistic behavior, to open yourself more fully to God's grace, and—most simply—to follow Christ obediently. It's in this spirit that Martin Luther exhorted priests who had precipitously taken a vow of chastity that they were obligated before God to forsake the vow and get married if they were plagued with uncontrolled desire.[3]

When Promises Should Be Kept—And When They Shouldn't
But what about promises made to other people? When are we bound to them, and when not? Here the problem is more complex. But we should start by remembering that, as children of Christ, we're ultimately bound not to promises but to the will of God. Under that will, of utmost priority, and second only to our call to love God himself, is our responsibility to love others for Christ's sake, and to devote our lives compassionately for their benefit. The question we must ask, then, is whether carrying out a promise will demonstrate Christ's love in the best possible way. There may be times when we actually love someone more effectively by breaking a promise than by fulfilling it.

I shouldn't think, for instance, that I'm helping anyone by carrying out a promise made, in a moment of weakness, to accommodate someone's immaturity or obsession to control my life. A deathbed promise is a classic example. Again, Martha Friedman comments,

> There is nothing basically sacred about the wishes of dying people. The act of dying does not necessarily give the ill greater wisdom. The dying may elicit feeling of sadness or anger or relief, we may or may not mourn them, but we are not obliged to execute their deathbed plans for us . . . . Far too many real life pledges have been carried out to the detriment of the pledger—and sometimes to others . . . . In some cases, dying people . . . who extract promises that their will be done are on an ultimate power trip. Just because people are in the process of dying, this

extremely common act does not absolve them of whatever living neuroses they may have had.[4]

We shouldn't feel bound, either, to honor a promise to a living parent, relative, or friend to take a certain course with our life—to pursue a particular career, for instance. The mere fact that someone felt compelled to illicit such a pledge from us indicates serious immaturity on their part. Carrying out the promise will only fuel their conviction they can manipulate others, and further nurture their need to do so. Our responsibility before Christ is to pursue a career and other major life paths that reflect the gifts and personality he has given us. Ultimately, this will also be the way we can best show Christ's love to others.

Other situations, though, are more complex, and require careful evaluation to determine the most loving course. John's predicament (the Kansas pastor at the beginning of this section, wrestling with whether to leave to his church) is such a case. I suspect readers arc split down the middle on whether he should have stayed or resigned. I personally believe the mix of factors recommended leaving. His sacrificial attitude didn't ultimately help these people. Rather, he allowed them to continue in a comfort zone that wasn't challenging to them spiritually. They needed to come to grips with their own needs for spiritual growth, and find a pastor who could truly nurture them. By sparing them the pain of looking for such a person, John deprived them of a healthy challenge they needed. And he also denied another church that would have more greatly benefited from his gifts the opportunity to do so. Yes, he set a heroic example to this congregation by fulfilling his term. But he would have served them better by confessing his presumption in making the five-year pledge, and admitting he would best help them by moving on. That show of humility would probably have benefited them more than the demonstration of sacrificial integrity (and underneath it all, pride of achievement) that he showed by staying on.

In other cases, though, our duty to love others requires us to keep a commitment we would prefer to break. Sandra, a young nurse from Los Angeles, agreed to travel with a missionary team to Kenya, on a mission requiring a two-year commitment. At the midpoint, her boyfriend Bill phoned and proposed, urging her to return home. Deeply homesick after Bill's proposal, and longing to marry him, she hoped the team would release her, and allow her to leave early. Yet when she discussed the possibility with the leaders, they reminded her that about a dozen others had committed to the mission knowing that a nurse with Sandra's skills would be on the team. They couldn't likely replace her on such short notice. In addition, if Bill's love was genuine, and his proposal worth accepting, he would certainly wait a year for her to return. Their relationship might even strengthen through the hardship. Sandra concluded she should keep her commitment to the team, and assured them she would stay. She told Bill she would marry him in a year, if he was willing to wait. It comforted her to remember a promise of Scripture directed to such situations: "O Lord, who shall sojourn in thy tent? Who shall dwell on thy holy hill? He who walks blamelessly, and does what is right, and speaks truth from his heart; . . . who swears to his own hurt and does not change" (Ps 15:1-4).

The Need for Faithfulness
This is the place to add a word about our need for integrity and considerateness to others, even when we haven't specifically promised our support. For many Christians, the problem isn't that they compulsively keep promises best left forgotten, but that they can't stick with any situation for very long. The freedom of movement our American society allows fosters such instability to a degree found in few other cultures.

Many Christians bounce from church to church, looking for the perfect Christian community, which of course they never find. Underneath it all is a fear of getting intimately involved with others, and an unwillingness to settle down and tolerate the imperfections of a given group of people. Accepting others warts and all is vital if I'm to allow a Christian community to benefit from my spiritual gifts, and if I'm to be a position where my own imperfections can be honed. Loving others for Christ's sake requires, in part, commitment to a local fellowship for a significant time. My own growth in Christ requires it as well.

Pastors and Christian leaders need to log substantial time with a given community as well in order to most effectively minister. I've known pastors who in their first years out of seminary have taken on new positions every six months or so. While they may not have broken stated commitments in these moves, they still have been less than fully faithful—to the people they have served, and to their own needs for growth. Even though most pastoral positions, and some missionary roles, do not require time commitments, it takes a settling-in period to discover how you can be most effective in a certain setting, whether it's a good fit for you, and for people to grow comfortable with you. It's hard to accomplish all this in less than a couple years, at least, and every situation deserves a fair opportunity to prove itself.

This principle proves true with most major life changes each of us make. We need to give each new venture a reasonable chance. We also need to be fair to those who are counting on us to follow through, and not change direction apart from a compelling reason. My point in this chapter isn't that we Christians have a license to be flaky, or to break a commitment simply because we would prefer not to fulfill it. Faithfulness, loyalty, persistence and stick-to-itiveness are vital virtues if we're to realize our potential for Christ, and make the impact on this world God wishes us to. I want, though, to liberate those who feel bound to a promise or vow that is truly wrong for them, that is hurting their effectiveness for Christ, and may be draining the life from them. It's here that God offers us the opportunity for a fresh start—and I urge you to take it if you're in this predicament.

"It is for freedom that Christ has set us free," Paul declares triumphantly in Galatians 5:1. He adds, "Stand firm, then, and do not be burdened again by a yoke of slavery." Any step we take that results in our feeling enslaved is not inspired by God. An unreason-able promise or vow we make can give rise to this sense of bond-age. In this case, our responsibility is clear: we need to do whatever necessary to gain release from our pledge, and to reclaim the spirit of freedom that should define the grace-centered Christian life.

Commitments that are reasonable for us, on the other hand, should be fulfilled, especially when others are counting on us to be faithful. We should remember that Christ has given us freedom, not for license, but that we might invest our life in the most productive ways for others' benefit. Each of us has a unique opportunity to be a gift to others during our lifetime. Discovering how we can be this gift requires a good self-understanding—a sound recognition of our talents and motivational pattern—as we've stressed throughout this book. It also requires a heart of compassion and a spirit of faithful-ness, as we seek to fulfill the mission Christ has for us, and bring his love to the people he positions us to serve.

Notes

Chapter 2: Taking Your Gifts and Desires Seriously

[1]C. Peter Wagner, *Your Spiritual Gifts Can Help Your Church Grow* (Ventura, Calif.: Regal Books, 2012).

[2]The New Testament also describes the Christian as a "new creation" (*ktisis,* 2 Cor 5:17), as having a "new man" or "nature" that has replaced the old (*anthrôpos*—Rom 6:6, Eph 4:22-24, Col 3:9-10), as one who is in the "spirit" and not in the "flesh" (*pneuma* vs. *sarx*—Gal 15:16-26, Rom 8:1-17, compare Col 2:9-15), and in terms of old and new "leven" (*zymê*—1 Cor 5:6-7). But a close look at these terms in context shows that they always convey the idea of one's spiritual orientation or moral nature, not the notion of psychological distinctiveness.

Chapter 3: Self-Consistency

[1]M. Blaine Smith, *One of a Kind: A Biblical View of Self-Acceptance* (Damascus, Md.: Silver Crest Books, 2012) pp. 59-60.

[2]Daniel Kahneman, *Thinking, Fast and Slow* (New York: Farrar, Straus and Giroux, 2011) pp. 82 et al.

Chapter 4: Seeing Your Limitations as Strengths
[1]Eventually, I discovered it was of Franklin D. Roosevelt!

Chapter 7: The Fear of Failure
[1]M. Blaine Smith, *Reach Beyond Your Grasp: Embracing Dreams That Reflect God's Best for You—And Achieving Them* (Damascus, Md.: Silver Crest Books, 2011) pp. 109-10.
[2]Paul Tournier, *The Adventure of Living* (New York: Harper & Row, 1965) p. 127.
[3]Thomas J. Peters and Robert H. Waterman Jr., *In Search of Excellence: Lessons from America's Best-Run Companies* (New York: Warner Books, 1982) pp. 141-42, 210-11.

Chapter 8: The Fear of Success
[1]M. Blaine Smith, *The Yes Anxiety: Taming the Fear of Commitment in Relationships, Career, Spiritual Life and Daily Decisions* (Damascus, Md.: Silver Crest Books, 2011) pp. 43-62. Smith, *Reach Beyond Your Grasp*, pp. 163-175.
[2]Judith Wallerstein and Sandra Blakeslee, *Second Chances: Men, Women, and Children a Decade after Divorce* (New York: Ticknor and Fields, 1990), p. 101.
[3]Martha Friedman, *Overcoming the Fear of Success* (New York: Warmer, 1980) pp. 159-68.
[4]Ibid., p. 191.

Chapter 9: The Fear of Commitment
[1]Steven Carter and Julia Sokol, *Men Who Can't Love: How to Recognize a Commitmentphobic Man Before He Breaks Your Heart* (New York: Berkley Books, 1987).
[2]M. Blaine Smith, Overcoming Shyness: Conquering Your Social Fears (Damascus, Md.: SilverCrest Books, 2011) pp. 73-78.

Chapter 10: Feeling Like a Fake
[1]Ibid, pp. 189-202.

[2]Joan C. Harvey with Cynthia Katz, *If I'm So Successful, Why Do I Feel Like a Fake? The Impostor Phenomenon* (New York: St. Martin's Press, 1985).
[3]Paul Tournier, *The Meaning of Persons* (New York: Harper & Row, 1957).
[4]Ibid., pp. 69, 80.
[5]Ibid., p. 78.

Chapter 11: Pulling Up Roots

[1]Peter L. Bernstein, *Against the Gods: The Remarkable Story of Risk* (New York: John Wiley and Sons, Inc., 1996), p. 294.
[2]Ibid.
[3]Smith, *The Yes Anxiety*, pp. 109-110.
[4]Thomas A. Bailey, *The American Pageant*, (Lexington, Mass., D.C. Heath and Company, 1956). The book has been updated frequently since then, with other historians participating, and is now in its fifteenth edition.

Appendix: Promises and Vows

[1]M. Blaine Smith, *Should I Get Married?* (Downers Grove, Ill.: InterVarsity Press, 2000), pp. 137-156.
[2]Friedman, *Overcoming the Fear of Success*, p. 75.
[3]Martin Luther, "The Estate of Marriage," *Luther's Works*, Vol. 45., pp. 18-19.
[4]Friedman, Overcoming the Fear of Success, pp. 74-75.

About The Author

*Blaine Smith, a Presbyterian pastor, spent 30 years as direc*tor of Nehemiah Ministries, Inc., a resource ministry based in the Washington, D.C. area. He retired the organization in 2009, but continues to use the name Nehemiah Ministries for free-lance work.

His career has included giving seminars and lectures, speaking at conferences, counseling, and writing. He is author of fifteen books, including *Emotional Intelligence for the Christian*, *Marry a Friend*, *Knowing God's Will* (original and revised editions), *Should I Get Married?* (original and revised editions), *The Yes Anxiety*, *Overcoming Shyness*, *Faith and Optimism* (originally *The Optimism Factor*), *One of a Kind*, and *Reach Beyond Your Grasp, Goal Setting for the Christian*, *Should I Wait in Faith or Step Out in Faith*, *Beyond Stage Fright and into the Spotlight*, *Turning the Page*, as well as numerous articles. These books have been published in more than thirty English language and international editions. He is also lecturer for *Guidance By The Book*, a home study course with audio cassettes produced by the Christian Broadcasting Network as part of their *Living By The Book* series.

Blaine served previously as founder/director of the Sons of

Thunder, believed by many to be America's first active Christian rock band, and as assistant pastor of Memorial Presbyterian Church in St. Louis. He is an avid guitarist, and currently performs with the Newports, an oldies band.

Blaine is a graduate of Georgetown University, and also holds a Master of Divinity from Wesley Theological Seminary and a Doctor of Ministry from Fuller Theological Seminary. He and Evie live in Gaithersburg, Maryland. They've been married since 1973, and have two grown sons, Benjamin and Nathan. Ben and his wife Lorinda live in Turtlepoint, Pennsylvania, and have two young children; Nate and his wife Melissa live in Medford, Massachusetts, just outside Boston.

Blaine also authors a twice-monthly online newsletter, *Nehemiah Notes*, featuring a practical article on the Christian faith, posted on his ministry website and available by e-mail for free. You may e-mail Blaine at mbs@nehemiahministries.com.

21761922R00115

Made in the USA
Middletown, DE
10 July 2015